PAINTING
Tiny Treasures

Cindi Gordon

NORTH LIGHT BOOKS
CINCINNATI, OHIO
www.nlbooks.com

ABOUT THE AUTHOR

My mother would say I started painting at age two, helping to "decorate" her walls. Being the first granddaughter and niece in my family, I received extra attention. Everyone thought I had the potential of a queen—until the next baby arrived. My Aunt Claire, however, continued to rave every time I'd paint a picture. So I blame her for my obsession, and thank her for putting me through the Art Student League at age sixteen. At that time, I didn't realize what a wonderful world of art was out there, I just had the desire to paint.

I began oil classes when I was thirteen and continued off and on throughout my early years and into marriage. After my husband and I started a family, I let my painting go. It was hard to find time with little ones on call. After five years of painting limbo, I signed up for a Rosemaling class being offered at the local community college. That was fifteen years ago and the beginning of a whole new adventure. Since then, I've read and studied whatever I could concerning folk and decorative painting. Using my former knowledge with these newfound skills simplified my painting, giving me more time to be creative.

The projects in this book are painted in a wide variety of decorative and folk styles, each a treasure in itself. I hope these ideas will help you to create your own "tiny treasures."

Other fine North Light Books are available from your local bookstore, art supply store or direct from the publisher.

04 03 02 01 00   5 4 3 2 1

Library of Congress Cataloging-in-Publication Data
Gordon, Cindi
    Painting tiny treasures / Cindi Gordon.
        p. cm.
    Includes index.
    ISBN 0-89134-992-8 (pbk. : alk. paper)
    1. Painting. 2. Decoration and ornament. I. Title.
    TT385 .G67 2000
    751.4'26--dc21   00-035497

Editor: Jennifer Long
Production Coordinator: Emily Gross
Designer: Wendy Dunning
Photographer: Christine Polomsky

DEDICATION

I would like to dedicate this book to the Lord.
Without Him I could do nothing.
He is the one who made this possible and answered many prayers.
"The Lord is my strength and my song and has become my salvation."
–Psalm 118:14

ACKNOWLEDGMENTS

There are so many people to thank; I wish I could name them all! I'll keep my list brief, but please know this is a small portion. Thank you so very much:

To my loving husband, Scott, for working so hard to provide for us, and for waiting for me to finish in "ten more minutes."

To my children—my greatest treasures—Trudi, Buddy, Ricky, Randy, Gretchen, Rita, Jeffry, Raymond, Gina and Danny.

To my dear parents, close family and relatives, for your love and support.

To my church family and friends who never stopped praying.

To the doctors and nurses who kept us all healthy.

To all the people at North Light who made this possible—especially Jennifer Long (for getting all of this in one book!), Kathy Kipp and Heather Dakota.

To my sister-in-law, Gayla, who's always willing to help at the last minute.

To my fondly remembered Aunt Claire (now gone) who started my obsession and never gave up.

And a very special thanks to my typist, Pam Holm, who spent many hours figuring out what I wrote and making it readable.

My love and appreciation go to all of you and to those not mentioned who stood by me, thanks again!

Table of Contents

CHAPTER ONE

Supplies

THE BASICS

If you are new to the painting world, start out with the basic materials. My supply list is only a suggestion, based on what works best for me; everyone has their own way of doing things. I also have a tendency to overdo it (you might notice), so don't feel you have to run out and buy everything on my list to achieve success in your painting; only practice will help you do that.

Disposable paper palette—This palette is very convenient—no preparation, no

cleanup. The trick to using it is to put out only the paint you need.

Spray bottle—If the paint on your palette starts to dry, mist it with water from your spray bottle.

Aluminum baking pan—If you need to keep the paint on your palette wet longer, mist the inside of a baking pan large enough to fit over your palette. Mist the paints, then invert the pan and use it to cover the palette. Acrylic paint will keep two hours using this method.

Small bent palette knife—Use the knife for mixing your paint.

Brush basin—I like the kind you can stand your brush in without bending the bristles.

Napkins and sponges—I keep a pile of napkins next to my palette for wiping my brush; this is easier than tearing off a paper towel. A variety of sea sponges

and kitchen sponges come in handy for clean up and faux effects.

"The Masters" Brush Cleaner and Preserver—I've found this to be the best brush cleaner. It comes in a cake; be careful not to rub your bristles too hard on it.

Wood filler

A variety of sandpapers

3M Sanding Sponge, Extra Fine—The sponge works well to smooth wooden objects between basecoats; you can also use a piece of brown paper bag.

Old white T-shirt—I cut the shirt into fourths and slightly dampen a piece to wipe off excess dust.

Jo Sonja's All Purpose Sealer—The sealer is wonderful to have on hand to seal almost any surface—an important step before you begin painting (see chapter three).

disposable palette pad, palette knife, brush basin and brush cleaner

sanding sponge, sealer and Right-Step Satin Varnish

J.W. etc. Right-Step Satin Varnish—If you added flow medium or retarder to your paint, allow twenty-four hours drying time before applying the varnish.

Tracing paper

White chalk

Stylus—Use the chalk, stylus and tracing paper for transferring patterns. The stylus can also be used to make small dots.

Chalk pencil—Use the pencil to draw designs directly on an object. Don't press too hard—you'll leave indentations and the pencil will be hard to remove.

Medium mop brush—This brush is good for dusting chalk off.

Pencils, pens, notebook and medium sketch pad

Bristol board—Use Bristol board or heavy cardstock to practice strokes.

Clear ruler—A 6-inch (15.2cm) ruler comes in handy when marking grid lines.

Tape measure—Small, skinny tape measures are the best.

Circle template—When making patterns, it seems I always need a circle. Use the template to get evenly shaped and correctly sized circles.

Scissors

Q-tips—Cotton swabs are great for removing mistakes.

Alcohol wipes—If you make a major mistake, alcohol will remove the acrylic paint, but be careful or you'll ruin your project. Try water first. I like the wipes because they're handy.

Non-alcohol baby wipes—I use baby wipes to keep my hands clean while working.

Jo Sonja's Flow Medium—I almost always add flow medium to my paint to keep it smooth.

Jo Sonja's Retarder and Antiquing Medium—To keep paint from drying in the ferrule of your brushes while you're painting, after you rinse a brush in the basin, stroke it through clean retarder and set it aside until further use. Clean the brush within ninety minutes.

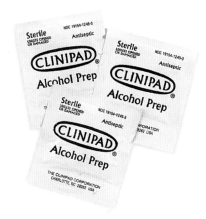

alcohol wipes

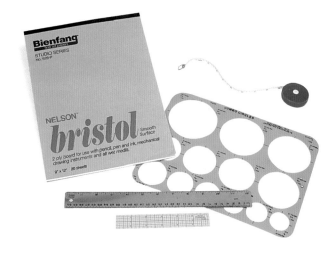

clear and metal rulers, tape measure, circle template and Bristol board

flow medium and retarder and antiquing medium

tracing paper, chalk, chalk pencil, stylus and mop brush

MORE HELPFUL SUPPLIES

I find the following items very helpful, but you don't need them immediately to get started.

Super Chacopaper—Use this blue transfer paper for tracing patterns onto light-colored surfaces.

Graphite paper—Graphite paper is good for tracing patterns onto other tracings; I don't use it on many surfaces as it sometimes stains.

Brush holder—The holder helps keep the brushes you are using from rolling all over. You want to lay your brushes down rather than stand them up when they're wet; the weight of the water will cause the bristles to spread out.

Winni Miller's Dry-It Board—This board really helps when you need to set a freshly painted piece down to dry.

Plastic bubble palette—I've labeled each hole in the six-hole bubble palette with a permanent marker for special mediums such as flow, retarder, kleister, glaze, blending, varnish, etc. That way I know what each is and they're not running all over my palette. Plastic works best—you can peel mediums out if they dry.

3M Long-Mask Masking Tape—This blue painter's tape is nice to have on hand to mask off things, or tape down without lifting paint (unless left on too long).

Paint pens—Extra-fine gold, silver and black pens are nice to have on hand when you need to sign a small spot.

EZ Dotz tool—A variety of small, uniform dots can be made with this dot tool.

Color wheel—Learn as much as you can about color and how it works.

J.W. etc. Painter's Finishing Wax—After your wooden project is varnished and cured, rub wax over it and polish for a smooth finish.

chacopaper and graphite paper

color wheel and chalk pastels

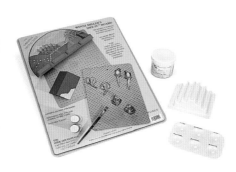

brush holder, plastic bubble palette, finishing wax and Dry-It Board

blue painter's tape, thin clear tape, paint pens and dot tool

Chalk pastels—Use with an old, dry filbert and sandpaper to create shadows and highlights.

Acetate

Blow dryer

Compass

Crayons or colored pencils

Glue gun and glue sticks

Graph paper

Index cards—I keep a color scheme file on mine.

Jo Sonja's Stroke and Blend

Jo Sonja's Kleister

Krylon Crystal Clear Acrylic Spray, no. 1303A

Krylon Matte Finish Spray, no. 1311

Lap drawing board with clip

Nail polish remover and cotton balls for removing paint

Old brushes for rougher tasks

Picture album with sticky pages for ideas

Plastic shoe boxes to organize paints

Protractor

Rubber gloves

Sponge brushes

Masterson Sta-Wet Palette

Strong glue and Aleene's Tacky Glue

Swing-arm lamp

PAINTS, MEDIUMS AND FINISHES

There are many varieties of paint out there. It's fun to experiment with them and hard to stick with just one. They all have unique qualities: thickness, thinness, great colors, etc. It's a personal decision on what works best for you.

There are also many mediums and finishing products worth trying; most are self-explanatory. If you are not sure of something, it's best to test it out first.

JO SONJA'S ARTIST'S GOUACHE TUBE PAINTS
These have a smooth, thicker consistency and come in a variety of colors, metallics and iridescents.

BOTTLE ACRYLICS
Delta Ceramcoat offers a large variety of colors and metallics. They have a smooth, medium consistency. DecoArt Americana and Accent each offer a large variety of colors and metallics with a medium consistency. Plaid FolkArt offers a large variety of colors and metallics with a medium to sometimes thick consistency.

JO SONJA'S MEDIUMS
Jo Sonja's Clear Glazing Medium helps thin the paint when painting in a layering technique. Jo Sonja's Crackle Medium creates an aged or porcelain look. Use Jo Sonja's Matte Finishing Varnish when you don't want a shine to your finished project.

GOLD LEAF AND ADHESIVE
Simple to apply. This is another way to add an extra touch to a finished project. Comes with complete instructions. (Also available in silver and abalone.)

SOFT FLOCK
An easy, elegant way to finish the inside of a box. It comes in many colors with clear instructions.

CHAPTER TWO

Brushes

BRUSH BASICS

Pictured here are the variety of brushes I used to create the projects in this book. This should give you an idea of what to look for and what each brush is best for. All of these brushes come in various sizes; choose the size appropriate for your needs.

Think of your brushes as tools. A carpenter couldn't get along with just a hammer; neither can one brush satisfy the needs of an artist.

¾-INCH (19MM) WASH
This is a flat wash brush used mostly for basecoating and varnish; keep one set for each task.

"DABBLE" OR SPONGE BRUSH
The sponge brush is great for painting along edges and in little corners. You can also use it to make some unique strokes.

NO. 6 BLENDER
Blending brushes can be used to soften harsh edges. To do this, it's best if your paints are mixed with a little retarder so you have some open time to blend colors.

NO. 12 POUNCER
This is a nice brush for creating faux backgrounds. It's not as stiff as a stencil brush so you'll get a more subtle look. Don't overload it; keep the colors soft.

¼-INCH (6MM) FILBERT COMB OR RAKE
The rounded edges on this comb make it easier to work around areas. Use this brush to create broken strokework, hair or fur. Load halfway up with thinned paint and use a light touch.

½-INCH (12MM) FLAT COMB OR RAKE
With the square edges you can create hair and a nice basket-weave look. Load the same way as the filbert comb.

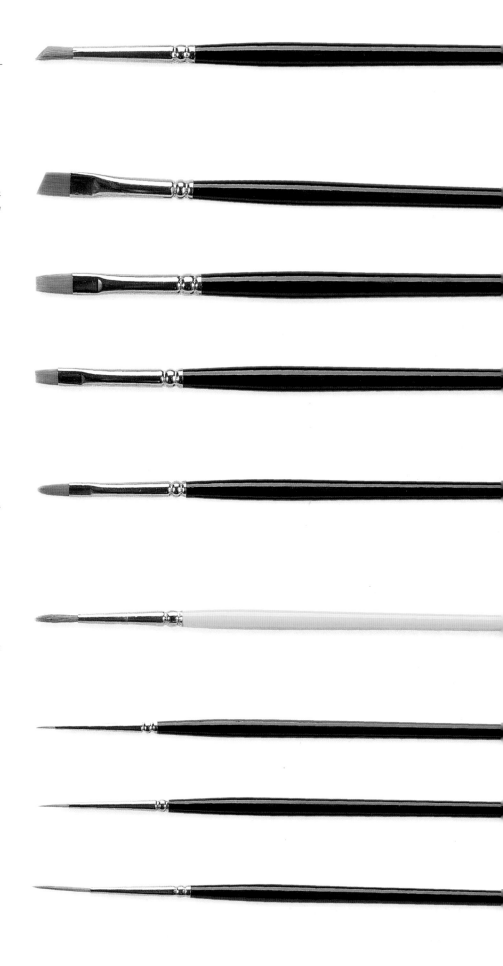

⅛-INCH (3MM) DEERFOOT

This brush can be used for all kinds of effects—a stippled finish, fur or foliage—or to soften a harsh look. Stipple wet-on-wet or blend from one value to the next. To do this, slightly load a dry brush, pounce on the palette to work in paint, then pounce onto the desired object.

¼-INCH (6MM) ANGLE

This brush is referred to as the "rose petal" brush because it's great for painting roses. It's usually double or side loaded to achieve beautiful color results. Also use it for S- and C-strokes.

NO. 6 FLAT

Great for strokework, double- and side-load techniques and filling in areas.

NO. 4 SHADER

Notice this brush has shorter hairs than the flat. Just as the name says, the shader is used for shading. The shorter hairs make this easier to accomplish. It can be double or single loaded.

NO. 2 FILBERT (OR CAT'S TONGUE)

The filbert is one of the easiest brushes to work with. The rounded edges help you make some lovely strokes. It's also nice for filling in small areas as it doesn't leave "ridges" like a round brush would.

NO. 0 KOLINSKY ROUND

This is made of the finest Kolinsky red sable, which will hold the paint well, creating the best strokes. With proper care, these brushes will last a long time. This is one of my favorites!

10/0 ROUND

These little rounds make the best small strokes and are great for detail work.

10/0 DRESSDEN (LINER)

Here's another brush I like to use for detail. It can be used for shorter linework and longer strokes.

6/0 SCROLLER (LONGER LINER)

Longer than the liner above, it is great for painting longer lines as it will hold more paint. Not recommended for strokework unless you are making long-lined strokes.

HOLDING YOUR BRUSH

If you've never held or worked with a brush here are a few tips:

- Hold your brush like a pencil at or just above the "crimped" edge.
- Extend your little finger to balance and support the brush.
- Keep the brush in a vertical position.
- Hold the brush in a relaxed manner, letting your little finger "bear the burden." In other words, if you feel shaky try to hang on with your little finger.
- Use your other hand for support by placing it under your brush hand.
- Sit in an upright but comfortable position.
- Think of your brush as a graceful ballerina, dancing across the stage; your strokes will follow. This might sound silly, but it works.

After a while, with practice, it will all fall into place. I don't paint the same way as other painters and neither will you. There's a common thread, but each person is built differently.

LOADING YOUR BRUSH

This is another important step in executing beautiful strokework. You want to have the paint properly prepared first. Mix the paint with a bent palette knife; don't use your brush to mix unless it's a very small amount of paint.

1 Pour out a nickel-sized paint puddle.

2 Use a little water, flow medium or retarder to adjust the paint consistency for what you'll be painting. If it's linework, you'll want to thin the paint to the consistency of thick whipping cream before it's whipped. If it's strokework, you'll want it a little thicker. For opaque coverage, you want it thicker, yet still smooth. Use the medium best for the type of look you want.

3 Dampen a clean brush.

4 Pull the brush toward you through the edge of the paint puddle. Don't gouge it into the paint.

5 Load the brush almost up to the ferrule.

6 Flip the brush over and repeat. You *don't* want to twist or roll the brush, but you do want to pull and flip the brush over until you have a nicely loaded, pointed brush.

Practicing Strokes

Now you're ready to try making a stroke. Practice on Bristol board or cardstock. You can also save your practice sheets for future reference (and for laughs!).

Where you want your line to be thin, lift the brush up onto the tip. When you want the line to thicken, apply pressure. Think "graceful," "delicate" and "thin–thick–thin." It will happen.

Keep your brush basin and a pile of napkins nearby and rinse and blot the brush often. Also keep your flow medium and retarder close by to adjust the paint's consistency.

DOUBLE LOADING

A double-loaded brush is loaded with two colors at a time, creating a nicely blended look between the colors. Double loading is usually done with a flat brush, but can be done with others too.

1 Moisten your brush with water or another clear medium.

2 Load one color on half of the brush, following the previous instructions for loading your brush. Be careful not to get this color in the other half of the bristles. If you do, rinse the brush out and try again.

3 Now pull the other half of the bristles through a second color.

4 Blend the two colors together in the center of the brush by pulling the brush in a back-and-forth motion on the palette, flipping over until you have a good blend. Don't overdo the blending or your color will look muddy. Don't underblend or your strokes will look striped.

TAKING CARE OF YOUR BRUSHES

You can't beat a good brush. A good brush is half the battle of making a good stroke. The other half is practice. Brushes will last longer and work better with the right care. Here are a few tips for giving them a longer life:

• Have clean water to rinse them in and change it often.

• While you are painting, keep a puddle of retarder nearby. Rinse your brush in the basin, blot it on a paper napkin, then dip it in the retarder.

• When your brush is wet, never stand it up; the weight of the moisture will cause the bristles to spread out. Always lay your brushes flat until they are completely dry.

• If you leave your brush in the water, make sure the basin doesn't allow the bristles to bend. Try not to leave the brush, especially a good one, too long in water; it will soak out the natural oil in the hairs, causing the brush to dry out.

• For me, "The Masters" Brush Cleaner and Preserver works best. When using it, stroke the brush over the "cake"—don't smash or rub it. Rinse thoroughly.

• For natural-haired brushes, apply a mild hair conditioner to the bristles after you've painted with a brush over ten times.

• If your bristles become bent, run them under hot water for a few seconds.

• If paint hardens in the bristles or ferrule of your brush, remove it with alcohol. Don't use nail polish remover on your brushes; it will weaken the glue in the ferrule.

• Have a different set of brushes for each medium.

• Don't keep the brushes in an airtight container or they may mold.

• To make a good stroke, you have to load the brush up to the ferrule. This is good for the stroke, but hard on the brush. When you are always working with a fully-loaded brush, be sure to rinse often.

• When you rinse the brush, lightly tap against the basin wall to knock the paint out.

• Use lukewarm water in the basin; warm or hot water will dry the bristles out and cold water won't clean the paint out of the brush.

• Make sure you blot the brush on paper napkins until the paint is no longer visible.

CHAPTER THREE

Getting Started

PREPARING YOUR SURFACE

Instead of repeating these instructions throughout the book, I thought it would be easier to explain all the preparation steps here.

Old Wood

Before you buy a wooden piece, look at the construction and check for knotholes. You won't always find perfection, so you may have to fix a few things.

If this is an older piece of wood with existing varnish, remove the varnish with thinner and a rag (wear gloves). Rinse quickly in warm water and dry off. Allow to dry overnight, then follow the steps for new wood.

MATERIALS – WOOD

- Wood filler
- Jo Sonja's All Purpose Sealer
- Variety of sandpaper
- Old T-shirts
- 3M Sanding Sponge, Extra Fine
- J.W. etc. Painter's Finishing Wax
- Variety of old (but not worthless) flat brushes (for basecoat colors)
- Variety of good, clean, flat brushes (for varnishes and sealer)
- Rubber gloves
- Paint thinner
- Medium-sized flat palette knife
- Piece of brown paper bag
- Jo Sonja's Flow Medium

New Wood

1 Fill all holes (including staple, nail and screw holes) with wood filler and a medium-sized, flat palette knife. Allow to dry completely.
2 Sand smooth with the grain, using fine to medium sandpaper.
3 Wipe clean with a damp T-shirt. I don't use a tack rag—it seems to leave a film that reacts adversely with paint.
4 Apply Jo Sonja's All Purpose Sealer to the entire piece. This will cause the grain to rise. When dry, the surface will feel rough again. Lightly sand with extra-fine sandpaper. Don't sand off the sealer, just remove the roughness. Wipe with a damp T-shirt.
5 Basecoat the piece with your color of choice mixed with a little flow medium to keep the paint smooth. Allow to dry.
6 Use a piece of brown paper bag or an extra-fine 3M Sanding Sponge to lightly go over the basecoat. Dust off with a dry T-shirt.
7 Apply another basecoat.
8 After you've completed the painting, varnished it and allowed curing time, apply Painter's Finishing Wax, then buff to a shine with a dry T-shirt.

New Tin

1 Using extra-fine to fine steel wool, create a slight "tooth" for the primer to stick to.
2 Wash the piece with hot, soapy water. Rinse well, then dry with a cotton towel. Let the piece air dry for a few hours.
3 Use the spray primer of your choice; there are many varieties and colors available. For beginners, I recommend getting a black primer for a dark base, a gray for a medium base and a white for a light base. Allow to dry.
4 Follow with a coat of All Purpose Sealer or Delta Ceramcoat Metal Primer. Make sure you smooth out the brushstrokes.
5 Apply the basecoat of choice.

MATERIALS – TIN

- Variety of steel wool
- Soap
- Vinegar (white)
- Old T-shirts
- Spray metal primer
- Jo Sonja's All Purpose Sealer
- Delta Ceramcoat Metal Primer
- Variety of good, old flat brushes (for basecoat colors)
- Variety of good, clean flat brushes (for sealer)
- Alcohol or nail polish remover
- Cotton balls
- Old, clean cotton towel

Older Tin

If the piece has a lot of rust, find something else! A little rust can be removed and further rust prevented, but beyond that it's not worth it.

1 Using medium to heavy steel wool, remove any rust.

2 If there is any grime or unusual film on the piece, remove it with alcohol or nail polish remover and a cotton ball.

3 Wash the piece in hot, soapy water. Rinse.

4 Rinse with a solution of half vinegar and half water. Dry with a towel.

5 Follow steps three through five under "New Tin."

TRANSFER METHODS

Chalk Method

Use on dark to medium-dark basecoat colors.

1 Trace the design (the basic outline only) using tracing paper and a pen or pencil. Cut out if needed.

MATERIALS – CHALK

- White chalk
- Tracing paper
- Small stylus
- Pencil or pen
- Mop brush
- Scissors
- Clean T-shirt
- Q-tips

2 Using the side of a piece of chalk, rub over the back of the tracing.

3 Center the tracing over the project chalk side down. Use a stylus to lightly transfer the design.

4 Dust the excess chalk off lightly using a dry mop brush; the pattern will stay.

5 When the painting is completed and dry, remove the remaining chalk with a damp T-shirt or moist Q-tip.

Chalk–Pencil–Chalk (CPC) Method

Use to trace onto medium-light to light colored backgrounds. The materials are the same as for the Chalk Method, with the addition of a sharp, soft lead pencil.

1 Trace the design to tracing paper.

2 Rub white chalk over the back of the tracing.

3 Place a pencil lead on its side and rub over the chalk.

4 Rub white chalk over the pencil. Slightly shake off the excess.

5 Follow steps three through five in the Chalk Method.

Super Chacopaper

This transfer paper is great for medium colors where neither the Chalk Method or the CPC Method would be visible. Use it just like graphite paper. Remove the lines after your project is dry using a damp cloth or moistened Q-tip—try to do this within twenty-four hours or the lines may become permanent.

CHALK PASTELS

This is a great way to create subtle shadows and highlights or to add a touch of color to your project.

1 Using the color of your choice, rub a pastel over sandpaper to create a little dust—you don't need much.

2 Rub the dust into the bristles of a dry no. 2 (or size appropriate to the area) filbert. Shake off slightly, then brush the pastel dust over the dried, painted project. If you aren't happy with the color, remove it with a damp cloth or a moist Q-tip.

3 When the right color is achieved, spray with matte varnish. You can now continue painting, or finish the piece with several coats of spray varnish and wax. Don't use a brush-on varnish over the pastels; you will remove the color.

MATERIALS – PASTELS

- Artist's chalk pastels
- Medium sandpaper
- Old filbert brush
- Krylon Matte Finish Spray, no. 1311

HELPFUL HINTS

Here are some tips and ideas that have helped me in the past.

Organizing Your Work Space

1. Use plastic shoeboxes to store each color family of paints if you have a lot of paint. Place these on a three-level, wheeled cart for easy reference.

2. Keep ten-pocket folders handy for notes and ideas to be filed.

3. Use index cards to record color schemes. Keep these in an alphabetical recipe box for future reference.

4. Collect paint sample cards from paint stores for color schemes.

5. Use sticky-page photo albums to organize ideas clipped from other sources. (These are great for clipped recipes, too!)

Practicing

1. Clip cardstock or Bristol board onto a clipboard to practice on.

2. Leave a strokework sheet in sight so you can practice before you paint.

3. Before painting a project, "brush sketch" it first as fast as you can. Then you'll have more confidence to paint the actual piece and you'll be warmed up.

4. Keep a record of mistakes so you don't repeat them.

5. Spend at least fifteen minutes a day doing strokework.

Time-Savers

1. Always have at least two brushes of each kind on hand in case one wears out during a project.

2. Have a trash can near your work area.

3. I keep an empty plastic shoebox on my desk. When I start a new project, I put only the colors I'm using in it.

4. If you draw a lot, get an electric pencil sharpener and set it nearby. Mine has saved me a lot of time.

5. Don't sit and wait for paint to dry; prepare for the next step while you're waiting.

6. Do two projects at once, keeping them in separate boxes. That way if you're waiting for one to dry, you can work on the other.

Preparation, Painting and Finishing

1. Sign your name on a piece of acetate. When you complete a project, use the acetate to find the best place to put your signature.

2. Copy black-and-white designs, then color them in with crayons or pencils to change the color scheme.

3. When transferring your design with a stylus, start at the twelve o' clock position and work clockwise around the pattern so you don't forget which areas you've already transferred.

4. When using tape to mask an area, paint sealer around the edges so the paint won't bleed underneath.

5. Always read through the instructions before you start.

6. If you're having trouble keeping your paint wet, add a little retarder to it.

7. Dip your brush in flow medium instead of water to keep the paint smooth.

Cleaning Up

1. Keep nail polish remover and cotton balls handy to remove paint from clothes, etc.

2. Use alcohol wipes to clean brush handles.

3. Baby oil will remove oil paint from skin.

4. Hardened paint in brushes can be removed with alcohol.

Keeping Kids Entertained So You Can Paint

Is anybody just sitting around with nothing to do—like your kids? Put them to work so you can get something done. (My kids love that idea!) Here are ten ideas for keeping your kids creatively occupied so you can have a little time to paint.

1. Kids always want to do what you're doing, unless it's the dishes! When I'm painting, it seems my kids all want to, too. I give my kids a piece of Bristol board and squeeze some extra paint out on my palette. Rather than giving them brushes, I give each child a moistened Q-tip for each color.

2. We have lots of drawing videos that keep the kids occupied. If you don't have any, they're worth the investment. Buy some simple ones.

A few of our favorites are *Learn to Draw* by Capt. Bob, *Cartoon Doodle* by Bruce Blitz and *The Draw Squad* by Capt. Mark Kistler.

3. My kids also love to paint on rocks. We have all the "Painting on Rocks" books by Lin Wellford (North Light Books). Even my little ones can paint a ladybug with a Q-tip.

4. Purchase cheap sticky-page photo albums and have the kids make their own "pretty pictures" book from old magazines.

5. Pick up some pom-poms (little fuzz balls), craft eyes and glue and let the kids make little animals, etc.

6. Have them make a book about their favorite subject. My girls love dogs and horses; they've made several books with cute stories. My sons love trucks and tractors, so they've made books about them. You only need crayons, paper and a stapler.

7. Have the kids draw pictures of you while you paint—this can be revealing!

8. My kids love making beadwork animals, key chains, etc. If yours are old enough, they'll enjoy it too.

9. Have your kids draw or paint pairs of objects on index cards to make their own memory game.

10. Play-Doh might be messy, but my kids love to use the rolling pin to make "cookies."

One more thing that kids can do is critique your work! Their truthfulness can be hard to take sometimes, but my children have pointed out some obvious facts.

Odds and Ends

1. Put your feet up on a footstool when painting, with your knees bent. This is a very comfortable way to paint. Since I sit at a desk, I just open the bottom drawer and place my feet on it.

2. Alcohol wipes are great for removing acrylic paint from polished nails. (Some polishes loose a little shine however.)

3. Don't paint in your pajamas—you may never get dressed!

TERMS & TECHNIQUES

You may find many new terms and "painter's slang" throughout this book. I hope this section will help you to understand how these words are used.

Antiquing – Antiquing creates an aged look on a finished, cured project. It is usually applied with a stain or a mix of retarder and paint, then wiped off to leave a hint of color behind.

Basecoating – Covering a surface with one opaque layer of color or varnish.

Blending – Joining two colors together evenly.

Blocking in Color – Painting a specific area of a design with a solid color using the biggest flat or filbert brush possible.

Brush Mixing – Mixing a color into a brush that has already been loaded with one color.

Chisel Edge – A stroke done with the tips of the bristles of a flattened brush.

Complementary Colors – Two colors directly across from one another on the color wheel, such as orange and blue.

Cool Colors – Blue is the coolest color. Most colors that contain blue are considered cool. Cool colors tend to recede.

Crimped Edge – The area of a brush where the handle and the metal section (ferrule) meet; a crimp holds them together.

Crosshatching – Rows of parallel lines that intersect, creating diamond shapes.

Cure – Allowing all layers of paint to completely dry.

Dirty Brush – A brush that contains paint from a previous step. When a dirty brush is called for, don't rinse the paint out; simply load the new color into the old.

Double Loading – Placing one color on one side of the brush and another color on the other side.

Dressing the Brush – Loading the brush with a medium or paint in a back-and-forth motion until the bristles are moistened throughout.

Drybrushing – Putting paint on a brush to which no moisture (water or medium) has been added to create a more "powdered" look. You can also use a slightly damp brush with a touch

of color, then work the color out a bit to create a softer look.

Faux – French for *false*. In decorative art, a painted finish that imitates the appearance of another material.

Ferrule – The metal piece that holds the bristles to the handle of a brush.

Floating – This is done by first moistening the brush with water or a clear medium, then dipping the corner of the brush in a touch of paint. As you gently "float" the brush over the painting, the moisture will cause the color to disperse and soften.

Freehand – To paint without the use of a transferred design.

Glaze – To apply a transparent layer of color over another color that has dried.

Hue – A color's name, such as red, orange or yellow.

Intensity – The brightness or dullness of a color. Usually pure colors are most intense or brightest; colors that have been neutralized or grayed down are duller. Don't confuse this with value; a dark value color can still be bright (Cerulean Blue), while a lighter value color can be dull (Ochre).

Lifting – When paint is removed from the surface, intentionally or unintentionally.

Linework – Fine lines produced by a liner brush.

Medium – Any liquid mixed with pigment to allow the pigment to be applied to a surface, such as water, oil, flow improver, retarder, etc.

Monochromatic – A color scheme using various shades or tints of one color.

Opaque Color – An application of color you can't see through.

Pouncing – Using a vertical up-and-down motion with the brush, almost like pounding but without harsh impact.

Puddle of Paint – An amount of paint squeezed out onto the palette to form a puddle.

Shade – A color which has been darkened by the addition of Black. I sometimes also use Burnt Umber.

Side Loading – Adding color to half of a moistened brush while leaving the other half clean to create a shaded or highlighted look.

Slip-Slap – Using a loose, back-and-forth motion of the brush to create irregular, crisscross strokes.

Stroke – A single motion of the brush.

Strokework – Basic decorative strokes, usually executed in a series of practiced movements, such as the C-stroke or S-stroke.

Swish – To loosely brush over.

Tint – A color which has been lightened with the addition of White. To get a very light tint, I start with a White base and add a touch of color to it.

Tone – A color to which gray or the color's complement has been added, lowering the intensity of that color.

Tooth – The graininess of a surface which allows the paint to adhere to it. A mirror has no tooth.

Transfer – Moving or copying a design to another surface.

Translucent Color – An application of color you can see through.

Value – The lightness or darkness of a color. Don't confuse this with intensity.

Warm Colors – Red is the warmest color. Usually when you add red to a color, it will make that color warm. (However, if blue is added to red the red becomes cooler.) Yellow is also a warm color; adding it to other colors can make them warm. Warm colors move forward.

Wash – Paint which has been thinned with water or medium, giving thin coverage.

Wet-on-Wet – Applying wet paint to a wet surface.

One, Two, Three Rose

hat is a "One, Two, Three Rose"? It's a rose that's as easy as "one, two, three" to paint!

Roses were the first thing to catch my eye when I started painting. I always wanted to paint one, but they seemed almost impossible. Even after a few folk classes on roses, I'd come home to practice and still get confused.

To make it easy, I came up with this rose. It's created with a double-loaded angle brush, using almost three strokes at a time. The process is easy to remember, especially for the beginner.

I hope you have fun with this rose and that you experiment with it a little. I've done this pattern on different colored backgrounds. A yellow candle also looks really nice.

The Candle

It seemed for awhile that candles weren't so popular—a candle store was rare. Now you can go just about anywhere and find a large variety of candles to choose from.

Giving unique candles for gifts always seems to go over well. Since candles have become so vogue, this set can be a great way to give warm wishes.

1 Wipe the candle with an alcohol wipe and allow to dry.

2 Seal the surface with Jo Sonja's All Purpose Sealer. Allow to dry thoroughly.

3 Using a ¾-inch (19mm) wash brush, base with Tapioca. Allow to dry.

4 Load a ¾-inch (19mm) wash brush with Icy White, then dip the corner in Payne's Grey. Add a small amount of retarder to ease the strokes and help with blending. Using a "slip-slap" motion, go over the base color, allowing some of the base to show through.

5 Trace the pattern outline onto tracing paper.

6 When the paint on the candle is dry, transfer the pattern using Super

SURFACES
- 3-inch (7.6cm) vanilla candle
- 2-inch (5.1cm) round wooden key chain
- 9" × 12" (22.9cm × 30.5cm) sheet of Strathmore 300 series colored art paper in a vanilla color, or a sheet of good watercolor paper

ADDITIONS TO BASIC SUPPLIES
- 2¼-inch (5.7cm) wide paper lace (vanilla color)
- Glue stick
- Small decoupage roller
- Thick cardboard
- Paper cutter (optional)

BRUSHES
- ¼-inch (6mm) and ⅛-inch (3mm) angles
- 10/0 Dressden liner
- no. 4 filbert
- ¾-inch (19mm) and ¼-inch (6mm) wash

COLOR PALETTE

FolkArt Icy White

FolkArt Tapioca

Americana Taffy Cream

Accent Crown Jewels King's Gold

Ceramcoat Light Timberline Green

FolkArt Gray Plum

FolkArt Metallics Plum

Ceramcoat Black Cherry

Americana Plantation Pine

Americana Payne's Grey

Chacopaper and a stylus and pressing lightly.

7 Follow the directions for painting the rose design.

8 Carefully remove the Chaco lines with a damp Q-tip or cloth.

9 When dry, spray with Krylon Matte Finish Spray.

The Bookmark

Since you'll be making your own bookmark, the size may vary. My bookmark is about 2" × 7¼" (5.1cm × 18.4cm). Art paper tends to curl when wet, so you'll have to tape it down; add about half an inch (1.3cm) to the length to allow for the taped margin.

1 Cut art paper to the measurements you've chosen (a paper cutter works best).

2 With blue tape, fasten the edges down on heavy cardboard, allowing 7¼" (18.4cm) between the taped edges.

3 Use a ¾-inch (19mm) wash brush to lightly wash on Icy White.

4 While the white is still wet, load the ¾-inch (19mm) wash brush in Icy White and tip the corner in Payne's Grey. "Slip-slap" across the white wash. Work quickly. If the base dries, remoisten and continue. Allow to dry.

5 Trace the pattern outline onto tracing paper.

6 Transfer the pattern using Super Chacopaper and a stylus.

7 Follow the directions for painting the rose design.

8 When dry, remove the Chaco lines with a damp Q-tip or cloth.

9 Finish with J.W. etc. Right-Step Satin Varnish.

10 When dry, reverse the bookmark to the back. Tape it down and follow the directions for steps three and four.

11 Remove the bookmark from the cardboard.

12 Rub the back with a glue stick.

13 Center the bookmark over your lace and press down with a roller.

14 Dampen a small sponge, dip in King's Gold and sponge over the back and top edges of the lace.

15 When dry, trim the lengthwise edges (use a paper cutter). Make sure the lace scallops are balanced on either side.

16 Spray both front and back with Krylon Matte Finish Spray.

The Key Chain

After you have accomplished the "bigger" version of the rose, you should be ready to try the smaller version. It does require a little more control, but it's not that difficult once you've mastered it. This pattern size is also fun to paint on an ornament.

1 Remove the chain and follow the basic wood preparation steps on page 14.

2 Base the front and back of the key chain with Tapioca using a ¼-inch (6mm) wash brush.

3 When dry, load the ¼-inch (6mm) wash brush with Icy White. Dip the corner in Payne's Grey and "slip-slap" over the background. Allow the front to dry before you paint the back.

4 Trace the pattern outline onto tracing paper.

5 When the paint is dry, transfer the pattern using Super Chacopaper and a stylus.

6 Follow the basic rose instructions, substituting an ⅛-inch (3mm) angle for the ¼-inch (6mm) angle.

7 When dry, remove the Chaco lines with a damp Q-tip or cloth.

8 Varnish with J.W. etc. Right-Step Satin Varnish.

9 Allow to dry overnight, then wax if desired.

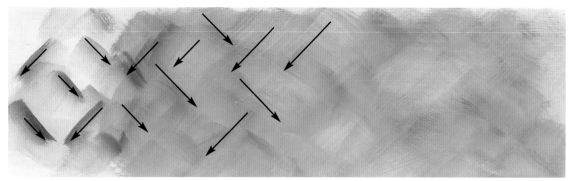

Add the Payne's Grey with a slip-slap motion, blending as you go. Don't overblend.

BOOKMARK/CANDLE PATTERN OUTLINE
Trace this pattern onto surface.

KEY CHAIN PATTERN OUTLINE
Trace this pattern onto surface.

DETAILED KEY CHAIN DESIGN
Use as a reference for placement of details; don't transfer these lines.

DETAILED BOOKMARK/CANDLE DESIGN
Use as a reference for placement of details; don't transfer these lines.

The patterns and designs on this page may be hand-traced or photocopied for personal use only. Shown at full size.

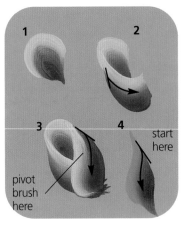

1 Small Bud
Double load a ¼-inch (6mm) angle brush with Taffy Cream in the upper half of the brush and Black Cherry in the lower half. Work the colors together on the palette so they blend but aren't muddy. Place the Black Cherry edge of the brush on the base of the bud, then pivot the brush in an arc, moving only the upper half. To make the calyx, load a liner brush with Plantation Pine. Start at the center and gracefully lift off as you end each stroke. Highlight the calyx with King's Gold.

2 Large Bud/Small Rose Center
Begin with a small bud (1). Reload the brush with Taffy Cream and Black Cherry. Pull a "weak" **C** from the left side of the bud. Reload the brush (2). Start at the top right and make a reverse **S**-stroke (3). Make a reverse **S**-stroke leaf with a double load of Light Timberline Green in the upper half and Plantation Pine in the lower half (4). Rose leaves sometimes have a little red in them; add a touch of Black Cherry to create this effect.

3
Load a liner with thin Taffy Cream. Starting where indicated by the dot on this picture, make a pointed oval to outline the mouth of the rose. Carry this outline into a sharp **C** along the front petal. Add the rose center with Black Cherry and highlight it with Plum. Add the calyx and leaves as you did in steps one and two.

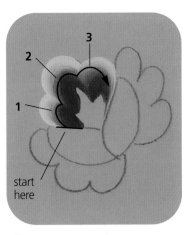

4 Open Bud
Make a large bud. Reload. Starting near the top of the left side, make a **C**-stroke (1). Pivot the brush and make another, larger **C** (2). Reverse the **C**s on the other side. Load a liner with Black Cherry and outline the center (3). Add the calyx and leaves as before.

5
To make this rose a little fancier, add Taffy Cream details with a liner as you did in step three. Add Plum highlights to the rose center and along the base of the center and a little King's Gold to the calyx. Now you're ready for the big rose!

6 One, Two, Three Rose
Load your brush as before with Taffy Cream and Black Cherry. This time you'll make three **C**s in a row. Keep your brush straight up and work with a light touch. Use the same kind of pivot you did in step four, only make it a little wider at the bottom.

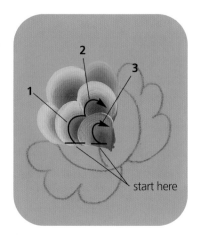

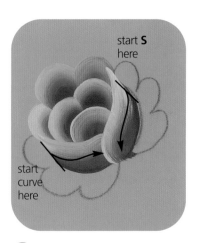

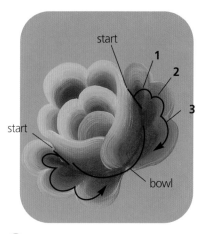

7 Reload your brush and pull two **C**-strokes overlapping the base of the strokes you made in step six. Overlap the base of these strokes with a single **C**.

8 To make the bowl of the rose, make a curve, then a long **S** with Taffy Cream and Black Cherry.

9 Reload your brush. Begin at the upper left side and pivot three **C**-strokes for side petals. Keep the bottom of the brush close to the bottom of the bowl. Repeat with reverse **C**s on the right side.

10 Reinforce the center of the rose by adding a darker circle in the middle using a liner loaded with Black Cherry. Strengthen the bottom of the bowl with the same brush and color; you can do this in two strokes or all in one stroke. Add leaves and the calyx as before.

11 This step is like putting the icing on the cake! Follow the tops of petals with the liner brush and thinned Taffy Cream. Start with a light touch at the base of each petal, then vary pressure to give the line character. Notice I've added extra petals in the bowl; I just brushed these in. Also, I didn't highlight the outer petals as it would be too distracting.

12 **Ribbon**
After you finish the design you'll want to add that extra touch with a ribbon. It's easy once you get the feeling of how to use the pressure on your brush. To make the ribbon, load a liner with thinned Gray Plum. Apply pressure, lift, then apply pressure again. Follow with Plum in the same manner. "Weave" the ribbon in and out of the roses. I added the gold edge by dipping a no. 4 filbert in King's Gold which I'd thinned a little with flow medium. Let the brush make the edge by standing up and pulling off. Do this on the key chain also.

Lovebirds

When I think of lovebirds, I'm reminded of my Grandma Marie and Grandpa Harry. Not only did they have a special love for each other, my Grandpa also loved birds. He always had a pet bird and would whistle to it every morning before work. My Grandma loved to have everything sparkling clean and nicely decorated. She got on a gold "kick" one year— anything that could be sprayed gold was—including the bird cage! She could hardly wait to present Pete the bird with his new home. Unfortunately, his happiness was short-lived, poor Pete! From then on, Grandma was often reminded of her "golden touch."

Something I didn't learn until later years is that my Grandma was a very talented lady. She used to make her own cards and had a love for painting. How wonderful to receive a handmade card, and how much more wonderful to have this precious memory from someone you love.

Handpainted gifts are little blessings you can pass down through your family to be treasured for years. I hope you have fun painting this and have someone you love to give it to.

The Papier-Mâché Box

Although you don't have to do much to prepare it, papier-mâché can be tricky to work with—sometimes it bubbles up and seems to show brushstrokes more.

When you buy a box, you also need to be sure your lid isn't too tight. The lid will "puff up" a little when you paint it, causing a tighter fit. Consider the fit and existing bumps before you purchase a box, but don't be too concerned. You won't find a perfect box; the bumps can add a little character.

1 To start this little box, carefully sand any rough edges.

2 Use a ¾-inch (19mm) wash brush to apply sealer to the entire piece.

MATERIALS

SURFACES
- Small papier-mâché heart box
- Various sizes of small wooden puffed hearts

BRUSHES
- no. 10 and no. 12 flats
- 10/0 Dressden liner
- no. 2 and no. 4 filberts
- ¾-inch (19mm) wash
- ⅛-inch (3mm) angle
- 10/0 and 0 round
- small sponge brush (dabble brush)
- ¼-inch (6mm) mop (or Suzie's Pit-I-Pat)

COLOR PALETTE

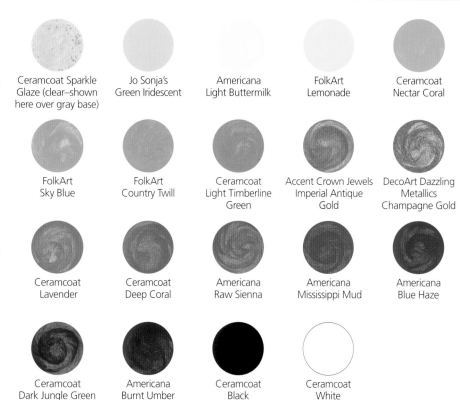

Ceramcoat Sparkle Glaze (clear–shown here over gray base)
Jo Sonja's Green Iridescent
Americana Light Buttermilk
FolkArt Lemonade
Ceramcoat Nectar Coral

FolkArt Sky Blue
FolkArt Country Twill
Ceramcoat Light Timberline Green
Accent Crown Jewels Imperial Antique Gold
DecoArt Dazzling Metallics Champagne Gold

Ceramcoat Lavender
Ceramcoat Deep Coral
Americana Raw Sienna
Americana Mississippi Mud
Americana Blue Haze

Ceramcoat Dark Jungle Green
Americana Burnt Umber
Ceramcoat Black
Ceramcoat White

3 After the sealer dries, apply two coats of Nectar Coral to the entire box and lid, inside and out, with a ¾-inch (19mm) wash brush. Allow to dry.

4 To give the inside of the box and lid a little sparkle, mix seven parts J.W. etc. Right-Step Satin Varnish to one part Champagne Gold. Cut a damp sea sponge into a triangle (to fit into corners). Dip the sponge in the paint mixture, dab a little off, then lightly pounce the inside of the box and lid. You can use the dabble brush to get into the corners if you wish. Allow to dry.

Give the inside of the box and lid a little sparkle with a mixture of varnish and Champagne Gold.

The Candy Hearts

1 Follow the steps for wood preparation in chapter three.

2 Basecoat the hearts using colors from this project's palette.

3 If you wish, use the designs on this page as a guide to decorate the hearts like little candies. The Dry-It Board comes in handy when drying small items like these hearts.

4 When dry, finish with Krylon Crystal Clear Acrylic Spray, no. 1303A since the hearts are so small.

CANDY HEART DESIGNS
Use as a reference for placement of details; don't transfer these lines.

LID PATTERN OUTLINE
Transfer this pattern onto surface.

DETAILED LID DESIGN
Use as a reference for placement of details; don't transfer these lines.

PATTERN FOR BOX BASE
Transfer only the grid lines onto surface.

PATTERN FOR INSIDE OF LID

PATTERN FOR SIDE OF LID

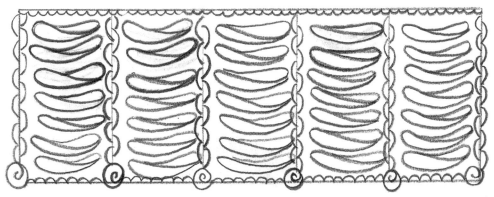

**PATTERN FOR WEAVE AROUND
SIDES OF BASE**

*The patterns and designs on pages 26-27 may
be hand-traced or photocopied for personal use
only. Shown at actual size.*

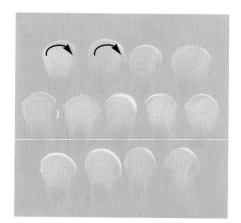

1 Top of Lid

Brush a light coat of retarder over the lid. Go over the retarder with a ¼-inch (19mm) wash brush loaded with Sky Blue. While the blue is still wet, lightly moisten a no. 10 flat with retarder, then load the top half of the flat with Lemonade. Working wet-on-wet, go over the blue with "windshield wiper"-like strokes, keeping the yellow edge at the top of the stroke.

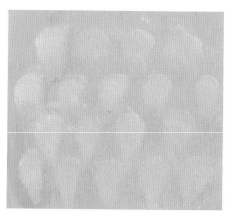

2 With a mop or Suzie's Pit-I-Pat brush, quickly and lightly pounce over the strokes you just made to tone them down. Allow to dry.

3 Use the pattern on page 27 as a guide for the scallops. To freehand, use a tape measure to evenly mark off the scallops—for my box I allowed ¾ inch (1.9cm) for each scallop. Mark the scallops with chalk. Using a no. 10 flat and Deep Coral, make **C**-stroke scallops. You may need to apply a second coat after the first is dry. Paint the side of the lid with two coats of Deep Coral using a no. 12 flat. When the scallops are dry, use a no. 10 or no. 12 flat to brush Sparkle Glaze inside the scalloped edge.

4 "Weave" on Bottom of Box

Trace the grid lines from page 27 onto tracing paper. Use the chalk method (page 15) and a stylus to transfer the lines to the bottom of the box. Brush off excess dust. Using a no. 10 flat brush loaded with Mississippi Mud, paint all of the horizontal lines, then the vertical lines. Load a no. 10 flat with Country Twill and blot on a napkin. Lightly drybrush this color over the previous lines, alternating from horizontal to vertical to create a woven effect.

5 With a no. 10 flat, drybrush Lemonade highlights over the Country Twill. Add defining lines with Mississippi Mud and a liner. Add Deep Coral shadows with a 10/0 round. When all of these areas are dry, go over the base with a ¼-inch (19mm) wash and Green Iridescent. Dry completely.

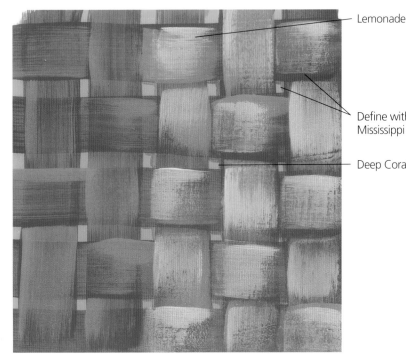

Lemonade

Define with Mississippi Mud.

Deep Coral shadows

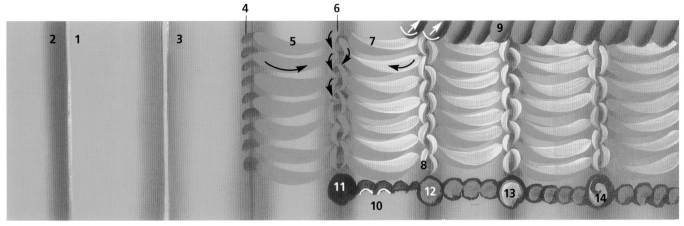

6 Sides of Box

This looks hard at first but it's really easy to do. Mark off vertical lines for the rows of "weaving" using a chalk pencil or chalk. Keep the lines straight (1). Moisten a no. 10 flat with retarder and side load with Deep Coral. Lay the coral edge of the brush on the left side of the chalk line and pull down. Repeat all the way around the box on the left side of each line (2). Clean the brush and then repeat the process on the right side of each line (3). With a 10/0 round and Mississippi Mud, make little eyebrow-shaped strokes along the center of each line (4). Turn the box upside down. With a no. 0 round and

Country Twill, make large eyebrow-shaped strokes filling the space between the lines (5). Turn the box right side up. With a 10/0 round and Country Twill, make sideways eyebrow-shaped strokes overtop the strokes on each line—these will look like chain links (6). To highlight the weaving, repeat the previous steps with a no. 0 round and Lemonade, pulling the strokes in the opposite direction (7). Use a 10/0 round to highlight the sideways strokes (8). Next, double load a no. 4 filbert with Sky Blue and Blue Haze. Lay the brush at an angle just below the top of the box and brush up and over the top of the lip, without going inside. Repeat

around the box (9). Load a no. 2 or no. 4 filbert with Blue Haze and make a row of half circles under the weave sections with the tip of the brush (10). Make a large half circle under each line. Go around the box, then flip the box over and finish the other half of each circle (11). Dip a damp, well-shaped Q-tip in Sky Blue and lightly highlight the circles (12). Add a second highlight to the large circle with Lemonade (13). Make a curlicue in each large circle with 10/0 round and Blue Haze (14). When completely dry, go over the sides with a ¼-inch (19mm) wash brush and Green Iridescent.

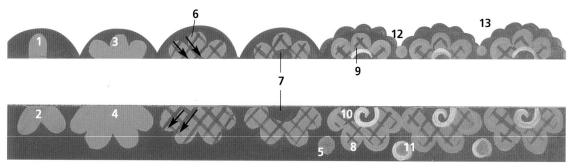

7 Finishing the Top Scallops and Sides of the Lid

We're going to make a flower that starts in the scallops on the top of the lid and spills over the side. This is fun and can be a versatile border, useful for many other projects. Load a no. 2 or no. 4 filbert with Sky Blue. Make a center stroke in each scallop around the top of the lid (1). With the same brush and color, make two strokes on the side of the lid under each center stroke (2). Now make two strokes on either side of the center strokes on the top of the lid (3). Next make another set of strokes outside the two strokes on the edge of the lid (4). Using the same brush and color, make little circles between the flowers you've just painted (5). Add crosshatching to the flowers with Imperial Antique Gold and a 10/0 liner—paint diagonal lines all going in one direction, then cross these with lines going in the other direction (6). Make a half-circle center for each flower using Deep Coral and a filbert. Paint the top half of the circle first, then paint the bottom on the side of the lid (7). Using a 10/0 round and Nectar Coral, out-line the flower petals, top then bottom (8). On the top of the lid, make a little eyebrow-shaped stroke over each flower center with Lemonade and a 10/0 round (9). Connect the eyebrow stroke to a curlicue in the bottom half of each center, using the same brush and color (10). Outline the circles between the flowers with Lemonade and a 10/0 round (11). Make small Nectar Coral circles between the flowers on top of the lid (12). Create smaller scallops around the scalloped edge on top of the lid with Imperial Antique Gold and a 10/0 round (13).

8 The Lovebirds

I left the background plain for this demonstration; by now you should have a beautiful foundation on which to paint the birds. Trace the pattern outline onto tracing paper. Use Super Chacopaper to transfer the pattern. Paint the branches with a 10/0 liner and Raw Sienna (1). Shade the outside of the branches with Burnt Umber on a 10/0 liner (2). Base the birds in with a no. 2 filbert and Lemonade; stroke these areas in, don't just paint them (3). Load a no. 2 filbert with Lemonade and stroke the brush on your palette a few times, then pick up Blue Haze on the side of the brush. If your brush gets too dry, add a touch of retarder before you side load. With the blue side of the brush toward the outside, go around the edges and wings of the male bird. Put a little of this color on his stomach (4). Repeat for the female with a side load of Nectar Coral (5). Start to add details to the male bird with a 10/0 round and Blue Haze (6). Add a few details on the female with Deep Coral (7). With an EZ Dotz tool or the end of your brush handle, make eyes with Sky Blue (8). Using a 10/0 round, make highlight strokes above the eyes with White or Light Buttermilk—Light Buttermilk will look softer (9). Add the top head feathers with Lavender for the male and Lemonade for the female (10).

9 Hopefully your birds are looking more like birds now. In this step we're going to overdo them a little. You don't have to get too wild; I love color and I do get carried away! Finish the leaves by double loading an ⅛-inch (3mm) angle with Light Timberline Green and Dark Jungle Green. Make little **S**-strokes. Add Burnt Umber to the branches and leaves with a 10/0 round. With Deep Coral and a 10/0 round, highlight the eyes, hair, wings and feathers. Start with a Black dot for the pupils, then add a little lash with a 10/0 round. Be careful how you place this or the birds will look like they're mad at each other! Add beaks and feet with Black. Using a 10/0 round, add as much detail as you wish. Use what I've done here as a guide.

10 *Finishing the Box*
Under the lid I have painted "2001" in scrolls; this is optional. It does look nice to paint something special under the lid. I used Imperial Antique Gold with a no. 0 round and a 10/0 liner. After everything has a chance to dry, go over the top of the lid and the lid sides with Green Iridescent. When dry, varnish with J.W. etc. Right-Step Satin Varnish and a ¾-inch (19mm) wash brush.

Little Girl's Trinket Box

Since the beginning of the adventure of writing this book, my younger children couldn't wait for another finished project. They knew there would be a few "rejects" they could have. The famous question was, "Is the next one for me?"

Children love boxes they can keep their tiny treasures in. I remember a music box with a dancing ballerina that my Aunt Deda had. It was so beautiful I thought I'd paint one for my girls.

As I was thinking about the kind of ballerina to do, the dancing pig entered my mind. She's actually my daughter Trudi's invention. One year Trudi made stuffed dancing pigs for a boutique and they all sold out. My mom was so impressed she gave the ballerina pigs as Christmas gifts three years in a row. Not realizing it, she gave a friend of hers the same pig each year!

The outside of the box is painted to look like a sheer doily. This is easy to achieve using a layering technique (see page 36). The use of the rake brush will help create the look of sheer fabric. Just follow along and you'll be happy with the results!

The Box

1 Follow the directions for basic wood preparation in chapter three; prepare the inside and outside of the box. If you purchase the card box, the wooden insert should come out for easier application. Allow to dry thoroughly or cure at least twenty-four hours. (You may want to prepare the smaller boxes at the same time.)

2 Using your ¾-inch (19mm) wash brush, basecoat the outside of the box with Ballet Pink mixed with a little flow medium. Allow to dry one hour—if it's humid, wait two hours. Open the box as each coat of paint dries so the lid won't stick. If the paint does cause the lid to stick, run a razor blade care-

SURFACES
- 7" × 4 ½" (17.8 × 11.4cm) card box
- 2-inch (5.1cm) heart-shaped box
- small pill box
- tiny bean pot

ADDITIONS TO BASIC SUPPLIES
- dark pink chalk pastel
- single-edge razor blade
- oval template (optional)

BRUSHES
- ¾-inch (19mm), ½-inch (12mm) and ¼-inch (6mm) wash brushes
- ½-inch (12mm) and ¼-inch (6mm) flat combs (rakes)
- no. 4 and no. 12 flats
- 2/0 and 10/0 Dressden liners
- no. 0 Kolinsky red sable round
- mini and no. 2 filberts (cat's tongues)

COLOR PALETTE

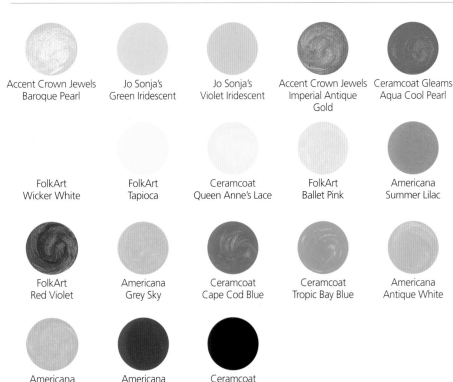

Accent Crown Jewels Baroque Pearl

Jo Sonja's Green Iridescent

Jo Sonja's Violet Iridescent

Accent Crown Jewels Imperial Antique Gold

Ceramcoat Gleams Aqua Cool Pearl

FolkArt Wicker White

FolkArt Tapioca

Ceramcoat Queen Anne's Lace

FolkArt Ballet Pink

Americana Summer Lilac

FolkArt Red Violet

Americana Grey Sky

Ceramcoat Cape Cod Blue

Ceramcoat Tropic Bay Blue

Americana Antique White

Americana Reindeer Moss Green

Americana Avocado

Ceramcoat Black

fully along the opening. Try not to force the lid open as you may pull the paint off.

3 Smooth over the box with a piece of brown paper bag.

4 Apply a second coat of Ballet Pink.

5 The next step is the glaze, which gives the box a sheer fabric look. Apply Jo Sonja's Clear Glazing Medium over the entire box using a ¾-inch (19mm) wash brush. This coat needs to dry overnight. Don't forget to open the lid. If it seems like a line of paint is forming under the lid, sand this off carefully.

The Small Boxes

I hate waiting for things to dry. If you're like me, work on the little boxes while you're waiting for the basecoat and glaze on the big box to dry. You don't have to glaze the little boxes, so you might be able to finish them while you're waiting. Prep and basecoat the boxes as you did the big box. I didn't include step-by-step instructions for painting the little boxes since they're pretty self-explanatory. Just follow the patterns and look at the colors I used. Don't get too picky, they're just for fun!

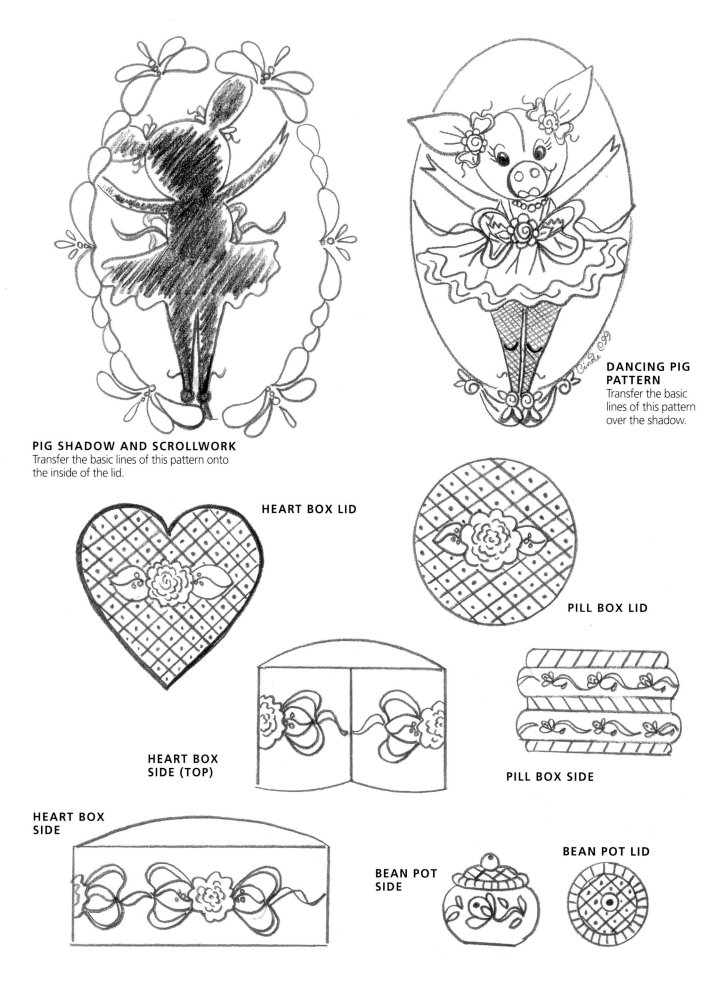

PIG SHADOW AND SCROLLWORK
Transfer the basic lines of this pattern onto the inside of the lid.

DANCING PIG PATTERN
Transfer the basic lines of this pattern over the shadow.

HEART BOX LID

PILL BOX LID

HEART BOX SIDE (TOP)

PILL BOX SIDE

HEART BOX SIDE

BEAN POT LID

BEAN POT SIDE

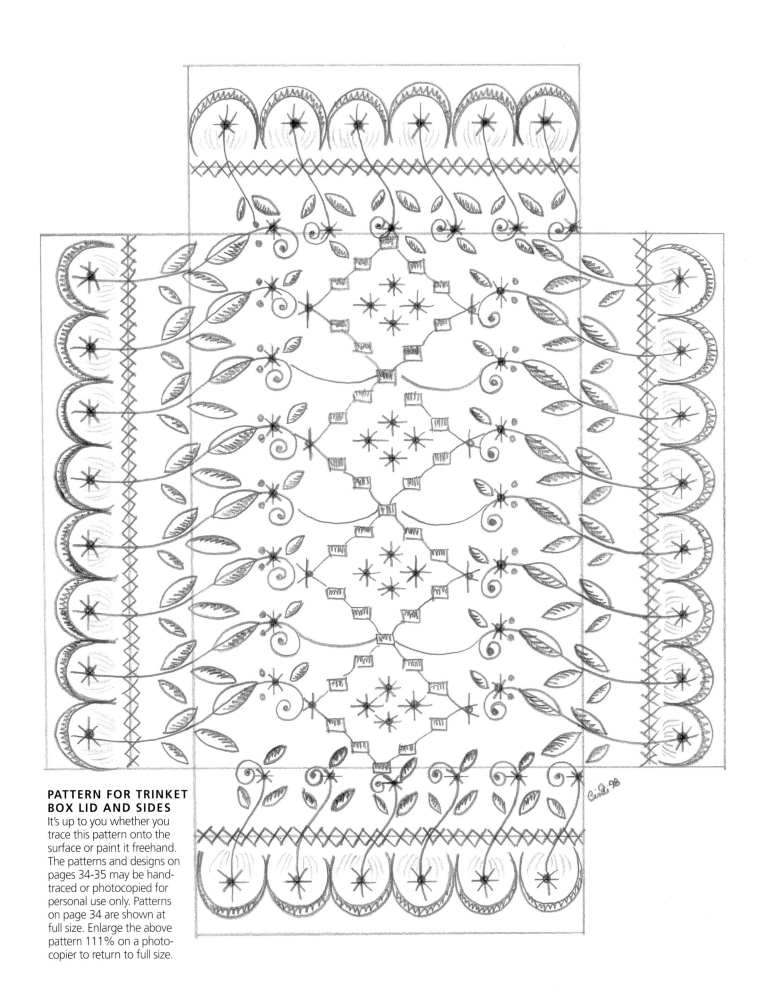

PATTERN FOR TRINKET BOX LID AND SIDES

It's up to you whether you trace this pattern onto the surface or paint it freehand. The patterns and designs on pages 34-35 may be hand-traced or photocopied for personal use only. Patterns on page 34 are shown at full size. Enlarge the above pattern 111% on a photocopier to return to full size.

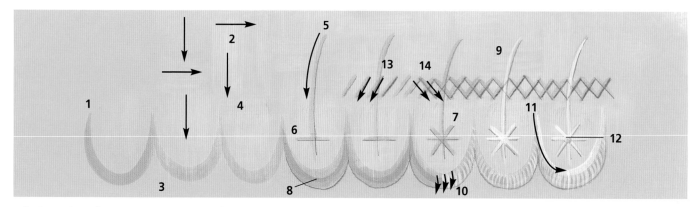

1 Creating the Woven Pattern and Detailing the Sides

Use the CPC method (page 15) to transfer the scallop design around the sides of the box. (To make it easier for you to see these lightly colored strokes, I've used pencil lines and left them visible.) Paint the scallops with a no. 0 round loaded with thinned Grey Sky (1). Mix two parts matte varnish, one part Baroque Pearl and one part Tapioca with a bent palette knife until it resembles cream. Dip the tip of a ½-inch (12mm) comb's bristles in the mixture and apply a random woven fabric pattern over the entire box with light, even pressure (2). Rake this color over the scallop edges slightly to create the look of frayed edges (3). Keep the pattern straight, but don't make it look like a basket. Work quickly as this paint will set up fast. This pattern should be very subtle; if you add too much color, it will take away from the lace pattern. Add "puckers" in the scallop areas with a 10/0 liner and thinned Grey Sky (4). Paint long threads in the center of each scallop using a 2/0 liner and Baroque Pearl (5). Turn the long threads into crosses with the same brush and paint (6). Add an **X** to each cross to turn it into a star (7). Use a no. 0 round to add Baroque Pearl scallops below but slightly overlapping the Grey Sky scallops (8). Add Wicker White highlights to the long threads and stars with a 2/0 liner (9). Add little stitches over the scallop edges with a 10/0 liner and Wicker White (10). With a 2/0 liner and Wicker White, add the top stitch line along the top of each scallop (11). Use the tip of your stylus to add a Baroque Pearl dot (12). Use a 2/0 or 10/0 liner and Baroque Pearl to make a row of diagonal lines all around the box (13). Go back in the opposite direction to make **X**-shaped "stitches" (14).

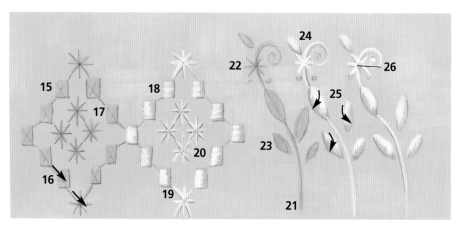

2 Detailing the Top of the Box

You will notice **X**'s under my square "stitches." I used these to represent the boxes when I transferred the pattern. If you are transferring the pattern rather than freehanding it, use the CPC method and be careful not to press too hard. Use a mop brush to dust the excess chalk off. The pattern lines should disappear when you stroke over them with wet paint. If not, go over them again while the paint is still wet. Be careful not to use too much pencil on the transfer paper or it will show through. Brush horizontally across all the square stitches with the no. 4 flat and Baroque Pearl, then go back and brush down vertically over the square stitches (15). Paint thread lines joining the square stitches with a 2/0 liner and Baroque Pearl (16). Form the stars as you did in step one, using a 2/0 liner and Baroque Pearl (17). Dip the tips of the ¼-inch (6mm) comb's bristles in Wicker White and lightly go over the square stitches (18). Highlight the connecting threads and stars with a 10/0 liner and Wicker White (19). Place a Baroque Pearl dot in the center of each star with the tip of a stylus (20). Extend the long thread lines from the side of the box with Baroque Pearl and a 2/0 liner (21). Add a star to each thread line with a 10/0 liner and Baroque Pearl (22). Paint the leaves using Baroque Pearl and the no. 2 or mini filbert (23). Highlight the long threads and stars with Wicker White and a 10/0 or 2/0 liner (24). With Wicker White on the tip of a ¼-inch (6mm) comb, highlight the leaves, following the direction of the arrows (25). Add Baroque Pearl dots in the center and on the bottom legs of the stars with the tip of your stylus (26).

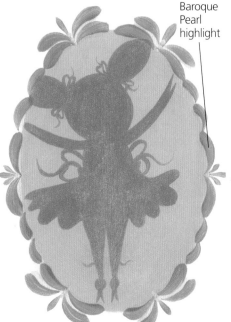

Baroque
Pearl
highlight

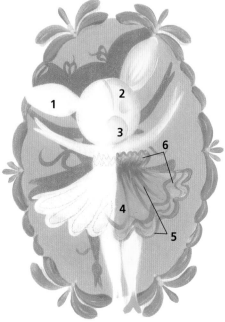

3 The Ballerina

To create the mirror, I traced an oval template with a piece of chalk. If you don't have a template, trace the pattern oval, cut it out and draw around it. Use the chalk method (page 15) to trace the pig's shadow pattern on. Fill in the oval with two coats of Grey Sky, using a no. 12 flat. Paint the pig's shadow with Cape Cod Blue, using brushes that fit each area.

4

After step three is dry, paint Baroque Pearl over the entire oval with a no. 12 flat brush. Use a no. 0 round to paint Imperial Antique Gold strokes around the mirror. Highlight the strokes with Baroque Pearl. Shade the highlighted area with Cape Cod Blue on a 10/0 liner. Create a shadow behind the dots with Cape Cod Blue on a stylus. When dry, dip the stylus in Baroque Pearl and go over the dots.

5

Base the pig with Wicker White, using brushes that fit each area (1). Allow to dry, then base the skin with Queen Anne's Lace (2). Float (see page 17) Antique White along the edges of all skin areas with a no. 2 filbert or flat (3). Base the dress and slippers with Tropic Bay Blue (4). Outline the dress and pleats with Aqua Cool Pearl using a 10/0 liner (5). Stroke Green Iridescent as indicated above to add an extra highlight (6).

6

Before you begin painting the facial details, add a pink blush to the pig's cheeks, inside her ears and above her eye area. Rub an old no. 2 filbert over a dark pink chalk pastel. Lightly apply this "blush" over the dry paint. When you varnish you have to be quick with the brush or spray—it doesn't take much to remove the pastel. Paint an oval for the white of the eye with Wicker White on a mini filbert. Make a smaller Tropic Bay Blue oval for the iris. Make an even smaller oval with Black. Use a 10/0 liner and Black to make the lid and lashes. Add a highlight inside the pupil and under the eye with Wicker White. Use a mini filbert and Summer Lilac to paint the nose and lips.

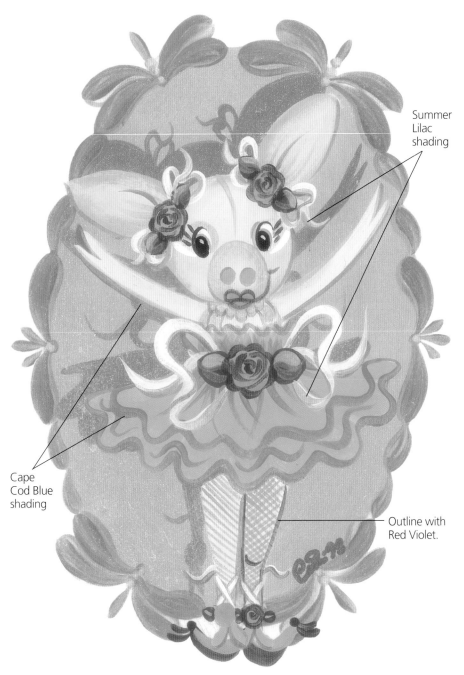

Summer
Lilac
shading

Cape
Cod Blue
shading

Outline with
Red Violet.

8 *Corners of Box*

Paint the inside bracket corners with Ballet Pink and a no. 4 flat. When dry, sponge with a damp sea sponge dipped in Baroque Pearl. Base the roses with Summer Lilac on an appropriately sized filbert, then go over them with Violet Iridescent. Base the leaves with Avocado. Add a stroke of Reindeer Moss Green with a 10/0 liner. Paint the leaf vein line with Cape Cod Blue.

7 Outline the lips with Red Violet and a 10/0 liner. Paint all of the ribbons and the shoulder straps with Wicker White and a 10/0 liner. Add the roses, following the directions for the larger roses in steps eight and nine. Using a 10/0 liner and Summer Lilac, add shading to the ribbons (except the ankle ribbons) and crosshatch lines to the panty hose. Outline the panty hose with Red Violet. Lightly shade various details, including the ankle ribbons, with a 10/0 liner and Cape Cod Blue. Dot in the pearls around her neck with Cape Cod Blue. When dry, go over the pearls with Baroque Pearl.

9 Use a 10/0 liner and Red Violet to stroke in the rose petals. Highlight the leaves with Green Iridescent and a filbert. Add the ribbons with Wicker White and shade with Grey Sky. Add Ballet Pink dots on the leaves.

I took elements and colors from the large box to paint the little boxes. Use the designs on page 34 as a guide, or create your own.

10 Finishing the Boxes

When everything has had at least twenty-four hours to dry, apply J.W. etc. Right-Step Satin Varnish with a wash brush. If desired, you can give the pieces a final coat of J.W. etc. Painter's Finishing Wax when the varnish has cured for at least twenty-four hours.

Tea Set With Berries

$\mathcal{I}$ bought this little tea set years ago and never painted it. Like many other "paintables" I've collected, I swore I'd paint it as soon as I got home—but life changed the minute I walked in the door. So down to the basement it went, with the rest of my collection. I've found waiting can be good. As the days go by our wisdom (hopefully) increases.

Berries were another of those subjects I took classes on at the beginning of my painting career. Since that was all I knew, that's all I did. At least ninety clay pots—and anything else in the way—got painted with berries. My husband asked, "Is that all you can do?" My reply was, "Well, I haven't taken a roses class yet."

Berries are still in style. Their color schemes have changed, but for something fresh, they're still a good pick!

This project is easy for the beginner. You should be able to freehand berries immediately.

Preparation

1 The surface you choose will determine how to get it ready. See chapter three for preparation instructions for the type of surface you're painting.
2 Basecoat the inside of the piece(s) with two coats of Lemonade using a ½-inch (12mm) to ¾-inch (19mm) wash brush. If you're painting an old piece, it may need three coats. Smooth with an extra-fine 3M Sanding Sponge between dry coats.
3 Base the outside with two to three coats of Sky Blue using the wash brush. Sand between coats, if needed.
4 Paint the handles, knobs and bottom of the piece(s) with three coats of Holiday Red. Dry thoroughly.

SURFACES
- Wooden sugar and creamer set with tray, or surface of your choice

BRUSHES
- ¾-inch (19mm) and ½-inch (12mm) wash brushes

- no. 8 flat
- 10/0 Dressden liner
- mini and no. 4 filberts (cat's tongues)
- 10/0 round

COLOR PALETTE

Ceramcoat White

FolkArt Lemonade

Ceramcoat Crocus Yellow

Americana Mint Julep Green

FolkArt Fresh Foliage

Americana Shale Green

FolkArt Clover

Folk Art Sky Blue

Ceramcoat Bahama Purple

Ceramcoat Blueberry

FolkArt Holiday Red

FolkArt Artist's Pigments Pure Magenta

Ceramcoat Raw Sienna

Americana Burnt Umber

Ceramcoat Black

FolkArt Artist's Pigments Green Umber

5 You can paint this design freehand or trace it on. If you trace it, use Super Chacopaper on the Lemonade areas and the white chalk method on the Sky Blue areas. Because the top of the tray is white and yellow, whatever you use to transfer the design will show through. Since this is just a background, I recommend freehanding the design. I know it's scary when you first start out, but practice and you'll be amazed at how easy it is.

❧ Hint ❧
You can save time by not waiting for all three coats in one color to dry before proceeding to the next color. Paint one coat on the inside, one coat on the outside and then one coat on the handles; then dry on a Dry-It Board for a half hour to an hour. Use your blow dryer on low heat to dry the paint between colors. Repeat for the second and third coats of each color.

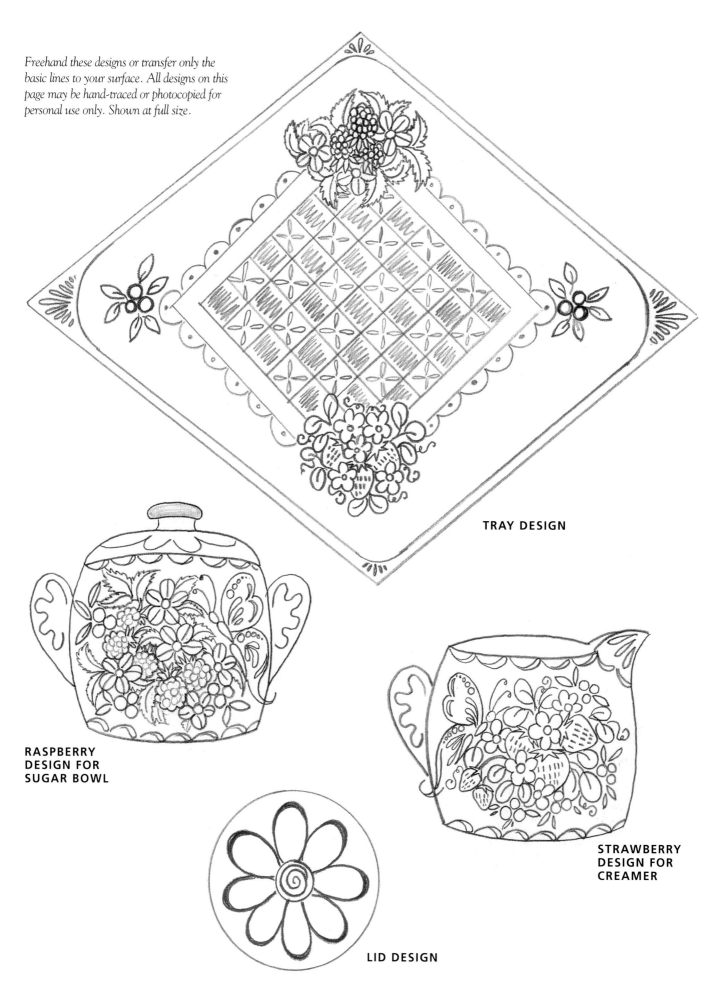

Freehand these designs or transfer only the basic lines to your surface. All designs on this page may be hand-traced or photocopied for personal use only. Shown at full size.

TRAY DESIGN

RASPBERRY DESIGN FOR SUGAR BOWL

STRAWBERRY DESIGN FOR CREAMER

LID DESIGN

1 *The Tray Top*

To create the diamond pattern, mix a little flow medium and White. Load a no. 8 flat with this mix and stroke back and forth until you have a flat chisel edge. Start in the middle of the tray and pull at a diagonal until you've got a diamond. Line up the right edge of the brush with the left edge of the previous diamond and pull another diamond. Work your way down in rows. Use a no. 4 filbert and White to make half-circle strokes for the scallop border.

2

Use a 10/0 round and Sky Blue to make the small strokes between the diamonds. Work in vertical rows, then horizontal rows. Use a 10/0 liner and Sky Blue to outline the scallops and add dots in the center of each diamond and scallop.

3 *Creamer and Sugar Bowl*

Before you trace the pattern on or paint any details, add flow medium to Shale Green and slip-slap a transparent background over the design area. Use a no. 4 filbert. Allow to dry, then use the white chalk method to transfer the pattern lines, if desired. Base each element in as instructed on page 41 before adding any details. Pictured above are the fully based-in designs.

Strawberries

Mix 1
Holiday Red +
Burnt Umber

Mix 2
Holiday Red +
Crocus Yellow

1 Stroke berry with Holiday Red and mini filbert.

2 Continue to fill in the base area with strokes.

3 Stroke shadows with mix 1, highlights with mix 2.

4 Deepen highlight.

5 Use 10/0 round and Bahama Purple for reflection. Add seeds with 10/0 round and Lemonade.

6 Base leaf with mini filbert and Clover.

7 Add shadow veins with 10/0 round and Green Umber.

8 Add highlight veins with Fresh Foliage.

9 Add reflective veins with Bahama Purple.

10 Add the strawberry stem with Green Umber.

11 Highlight the stem with Fresh Foliage.

Raspberries

Mix 1
Pure Magenta
+ Black

Mix 2
Pure Magenta
+ White

Mix 3
Mix 2 + more
White

1 Stroke berry with Pure Magenta and mini filbert.

2 Fill in the base area with more strokes.

3 Add shadow with mix 1.

4 With 10/0 round and mix 2, add seeds.

5 Outline berry with mix 1. Highlight seeds with mix 3.

6 Add Bahama Purple reflection with 10/0 round. Brush a little Holiday Red mixed with Kleister over the berry to make it redder.

7 Use mini filbert and Clover to make leaf strokes.

8 Highlight with Fresh Foliage.

9 Add shadow veins and lines with a 10/0 round and Green Umber.

10 Highlight with Mint Julep Green. Add the reflection with Bahama Purple.

11 Add the raspberry stem with Green Umber.

12 Highlight the stem with Mint Julep Green.

Blueberries

Mix 1
Blueberry +
Black

Mix 2
Blueberry +
White

Mix 3
Bahama Purple + White

1 Base the berry with mix 2 on a mini filbert.

2 Use a mini filbert to stroke Bahama Purple over the base.

3 Pull a stroke of mix 3 down across the Bahama Purple.

4 With a 10/0 round and mix 1, shade the side and bottom.

5 Use a 10/0 round to start the blueberry leaf with strokes of Green Umber.

6 Fill in the base areas with another stroke.

7 Highlight the leaf with Mint Julep Green.

8 Paint the stem with a double load of Burnt Umber and Raw Sienna.

Blossoms

Mix 1
Bahama Purple + White

1 Use mix 1 and a mini filbert to stroke the petals in.

2 Highlight the petals with White using a 10/0 round. Add a Crocus Yellow dot for the center.

3 Shade with Bahama Purple. Add the stamen with a small stylus and Clover.

Mix 2
Pure Magenta + White

Mix 3
Mix 2 + more White

1 Base the petals with mix 2 and the mini filbert. Add Pure Magenta shadows with a 10/0 round. Stroke in mix 3 highlights.

2 Outline the petals with mix 3 on a 10/0 round. Add a Lemonade center.

3 Make the stamen with a small stylus and Fresh Foliage. Use Pure Magenta for the center dot.

Butterflies

Mix 1
Mint Julep Green + White

1 Base the wings with the mini filbert and Lemonade. Stroke the body in with a 10/0 round and Burnt Umber. Add strokes of Mint Julep Green and Bahama Purple to the wings.

2 With a 10/0 round overstroke the green with White. Add reflections to the body with Bahama Purple. Use the small stylus to add Bahama Purple dots.

1 Base the other butterfly's wings with mix 1. Add the body as before. Add strokes of Lemonade and Bahama Purple to the wings.

2 With a 10/0 round, add White overstrokes. Add reflections and dots as before.

Finishing

When you've completed the set and have allowed enough drying time, dust it off with a mop brush and spray with Krylon Crystal Clear Acrylic Spray, no. 1303A. If you would like an even smoother finish, after it has cured for at least twenty-four hours you can add J.W. etc. Painter's Finishing Wax. Now you can paint berries on everything!

Swedish Plates

I have Swedish heritage from both my dad and mom. It didn't seem that important growing up, although a special trunk was handed down to me from Sweden. "Gramzy" told me a few times I should paint it because it was so plain. Now that I've had the chance to study the various styles of folk painting, I'm glad I didn't. I may have covered it with berries.

This isn't a true Swedish Dala painting because of the colors I chose. With such a small area to work in, too many colors could have been confusing. Since we're working with small plates, I thought it would be fun to do a red-and-white and a blue-and-white version.

On pages 50-51 you'll see the strokes and motifs I've used. Theses are the same used in Dalmålning, although I've made them a little heavier.

Creating a Porcelain Finish

With this project you'll want to achieve as smooth a surface as possible. We're going for a porcelain look. This is hard since we're brushing the basecoat onto wood. Creating a porcelain finish requires a lot of waiting; you might want to work on another project or practice your strokework between dry times. Even though this method of basecoating seems like a hassle, it will improve your painting skill—so try it! If you're pressed for time, use Krylon Satin Antique White spray paint to basecoat the plates.

1 Prepare the plates following the instructions for basic wood prep on page 14. If you want to use the Antique

SURFACES
- two 6-inch (15.2cm) diameter flat-rim wooden plates

ADDITIONS TO BASIC SUPPLIES
- four pieces of white cotton cloth
- Krylon Satin spray paint, Antique White no. 1503 (optional)

BRUSHES
- ¾-inch (19mm) wash brush
- no. 0 and no. 2 flats
- 10/0 Dressden liner
- no. 2 filbert (cat's tongue)
- 10/0 and 2/0 rounds

COLOR PALETTE

FolkArt Warm White   Ceramcoat Antique Rose   Ceramcoat Black Cherry   FolkArt Porcelain Blue   Americana Deep Midnight Blue

White spray, you can do it now. Give the plates at least two to three even coats. Once dry, you can skip to step 13.

2 To get the right look you need the right paint mix. Put a puddle of Warm White on the palette, then add equal parts of flow medium and water a few drops at a time (if you add all flow medium it slows the drying time down and the basecoat is not as hard). Mix with a palette knife until smooth and creamy. Don't make it too thin or it won't cover well; too thick and it will leave ridges and be hard to work with.

3 Work your paint into a ¾-inch (19mm) wash brush and stroke on the palette until your bristles form a chisel edge. Go completely around the inner top edge of the plate. Try to keep the paint on your brush balanced.

4 Working quickly, start from the center of the plate and stroke horizontally to

the rim. Blend all of the strokes together, lifting off as you near the edge.

5 Work on the rim next. Position your brush on the outside edge, then brush in horizontally. Don't brush from the inside out or you'll get a ridge. Work across the top and bottom, keeping the strokes even. Don't worry if there are a few small ridges, you'll be sanding between coats and the small ones will come off. When the entire top of the plate is done, let it dry one hour.

6 Place the plate face down on a dry white cotton cloth (handle it with the cloth also). This will keep it from getting marked or scratched.

7 With the same paint mixture and brush, start on the outside and go around the rim. Keep the paint even and at the right consistency. You'll get the feel of it with practice.

8 Go over the bottom with smooth, horizontal strokes.

9 Allow to dry at least one hour.

10 Cut an extra-fine 3M Sanding Sponge into a 2" × 2" (5.1cm × 5.1cm) square, then cut the square in half.

11 Sand very lightly over the entire plate. Wipe with a damp white cotton cloth to remove dust.

12 Repeat the entire basecoating procedure two more times, except don't sand after the final coat of paint.

13 If you want to add extra protection from unwanted marks or mistakes during painting, spray the plate with Krylon Matte Finish Spray, no. 1311 when the plate is completely dry. There is a drawback to spraying the plates now—the painting on it may be more transparent. Allow the basecoat to cure at least twenty-four hours before you start your design.

RED-AND-WHITE PLATE DESIGN

The designs on pages 48-49 may be hand-traced or photocopied for personal use only. Shown at full size.

Transferring the Design

1 Trace the main lines of the design (not the details) to tracing paper.

2 Cut along the outer edge of the circle, then make one cut in and carefully cut out the inner circle. This will make it easier to trace the pattern onto the plate.

3 Use the CPC method (page 15) to transfer the inside pattern to the plate. Tape it down with a small piece of 3M Long-Mask Masking Tape and lightly trace over the lines with a stylus.

4 Paint the inside as instructed on the following pages. When this is dry, transfer the rim pattern with the CPC method. Dust off.

BLUE-AND-WHITE PLATE DESIGN

Practice Worksheet for Red-and-White Plate

Using the brush listed below each element, follow the
arrows to practice creating each stroke. These strokes make
up the plate designs.

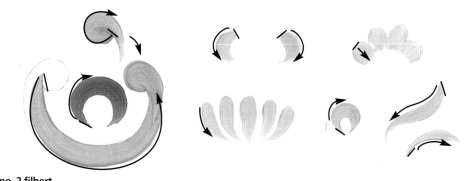

no. 2 filbert

no. 0 flat

10/0 Dressden liner

10/0 round

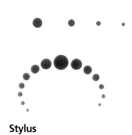

Stylus

2/0 round

Mix 1
touch Antique
Rose to quarter-size
puddle of Kleister

Mix 2
3 parts Kleister to 1
part Antique Rose

Practice Worksheet for Blue-and-White Plate

Using the brush listed below each element, follow the arrows to practice creating each stroke. These strokes make up the plate designs.

Mix 1
1 part Kleister to 1 part Porcelain Blue; mix with palette knife.

no. 2 filbert or no. 0 flat
Use mix 1 to fill in bottom of clouds quickly and lightly. If this color is too heavy, the clouds won't appear to be in the background.

10/0 round – "Sketch" top of clouds, getting smaller as you near bottom.

Mix 2
1 part Porcelain Blue to 1 part Deep Midnight Blue + a little flow medium; mix with palette knife.

10/0 liner

no. 2 filbert – Use mix 1 to lightly tap in the background trees and sketch the shore lines.

no. 2 filbert and 10/0 round
Add shadows with mix 2.

10/0 round
Base trunk with mix 2. "Sketch" in leaves and shadows with mix 1. Deepen with mix 2.

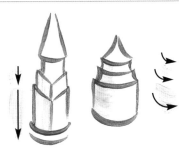

10/0 liner or round
Line in mix 2.

no. 2 filbert or no. 0 flat
Use mix 1 for the shadows.

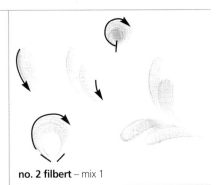

no. 2 filbert – mix 1

Mix 3
1 part Warm White to 1 part Porcelain Blue + a little flow medium. Mix with palette knife.

10/0 liner – Deep Midnight Blue and a little flow medium. These **V**-shaped strokes are called "spanners." They hold the floral sprays together.

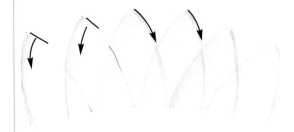

no. 2 flat – For the top rim of plate, start at top with mix 3 and go around plate.
10/0 liner – Go around plate again making thin lines.

10/0 round
small details

10/0 liner
crosshatching and large details

stylus for dots

1 Basing in the Inside of the Red-and-White Plate

Using mix 1 (page 50) base in the elements on the *inside* of the plate only. Although all basing steps are shown here, you will complete the design on the inside first so you don't have to handle the rim after you paint it. Refer to the worksheet on page 50 for brush sizes and help with the strokes. Finish basing with mix 2.

2 Detailing the Inside of the Red-and-White Plate

Follow the detailed design on page 48 to paint the linework using Black Cherry thinned with flow medium. If you mess up on a stroke, wipe it with a damp Q-tip quickly—Black Cherry will stain if left too long, especially if you didn't spray the plate with Krylon Matte Finish. This step is shown completed on page 53.

3 Basing the Rim of the Red-and-White Plate

Base the rim elements as you did the inside elements, referring to page 50 for brush sizes and stroke guides.

4 Finishing the Red-and-White Plate

Finish the rim linework as shown. Work one stroke all the way around the plate before you begin the next. After you complete all the details, dampen a sea sponge with 3 parts Kleister to 1 part Antique Rose. Test first on scrap paper. Starting from the design, sponge to the edge. When this is thoroughly dry, use a cotton cloth to hold the plate in your hand and sponge the bottom as you did the top rim.

5 Finger Rolling

Brush the back of the rim with mix 2 on a ¾-inch (19mm) wash brush. Paint 2 inches (5.1cm) at a time. Place your pinky over the wet paint and roll back and forth, then lift. Repeat all around the rim (see right). Allow the plate to cure twenty-four hours on a Dry-It Board, then dust with a mop brush or damp cloth and spray with Krylon Crystal Clear Acrylic Spray, no. 1303A. Wax after twenty-four hours, if desired.

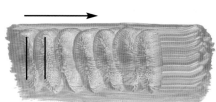

1 Painting the Inside of the Blue-and-White Plate

If you are planning to transfer the city onto the plate, first paint the background clouds as shown on page 51. Dry, then transfer the main lines of the pattern. Again, complete the inside pattern first before starting the rim. To paint the city, first outline it with mix 2 (page 51). Also paint the tree trunks with this mix. Don't do the flowers (called a "Kurbit") yet, save that for when the city is done. Use mix 2 for the background elements and straight Deep Midnight Blue for the foreground elements. Add the shadows as shown. Continue to add details until the city is finished, as shown on page 55. Allow to dry. Pour a puddle of Glazing Medium the size of a quarter and add a touch of Porcelain Blue to it. Give the city a wash of this mix (see next page). This will push it further into the background. Use a ¼-inch (19mm) wash brush to do this.

Sponge between **V**s

2 Finishing the Blue-and-White Plate

To do the Kurbit, start with the shadow using mix 3 (page 51). Add the details with Deep Midnight Blue, starting with the spanner (**V**-shape under the flowers) and working your way around. When you've finished the inside of the plate, start the top rim of the plate by lightly using the CPC method to transfer the pattern. Don't add the four floral sprays yet—

wait until the background lines are done. Refer to the worksheet on page 51 to paint the pattern lines on the rim.

Now you're ready for the rim florals. Use Deep Midnight Blue and a 10/0 liner and 10/0 round brush. The four steps that make up these florals are shown above. Sponge the rim with a damp sea sponge and mix 3 as shown above. When completely dry, turn the plate over, using a white cotton cloth to hold

it. Sponge over the bottom of the plate. Add the finger roll as you did for the red-and-white plate, using mix 3 and a ¾-inch (19mm) wash brush. After you've finished the painting, allow to cure twenty-four hours on a Dry-It Board. Then dust with a mop brush or damp white cloth and spray with Krylon Crystal Clear Acrylic Spray, no. 1303A. If desired, wax after another twenty-four hours.

Compact and Comb

*othing is more feminine in a lady's purse then her compact. It's something personal she uses to add that last touch just before facing the world.

My daughter Trudi and I love to look for compacts at antique shows. We're both amazed at their construction and beauty. You don't find that often these days, especially in common places. I did, however, find a plain compact in a common place—a dollar store! When I saw it I thought, "Wow, it's wooden; it can be painted!" So a few came home and were transformed. What a lot of fun you can have when you see hidden potential.

The Comb

1 Sand the comb. Using 3M Long-Mask Masking Tape, mask off the teeth and just above the teeth—only the upper edge should be showing. Apply Jo Sonja's All-Purpose Sealer to the exposed edge. Set aside to dry.
2 Spray the exposed edge with two thin coats of Black Satin Krylon. Allow to dry.
3 Paint the top of the comb with a no. 8 flat and two coats of Sequin Black. Remove the tape when dry.

The Compact

1 Cut a piece of contact paper larger than the mirror. Peel off the backing and apply the contact paper to the mirror, then trim to fit the mirror with a razor blade.
2 Use Scotch tape to mask off the edges that touch each other when the compact is closed.

SURFACES
- wooden compact and comb

ADDITIONS TO BASIC SUPPLIES
- small piece of contact paper
- single-edge razor blade
- permanent black marker
- Krylon Satin spray paint, Black

BRUSHES
- ¾-inch (19mm) or 1-inch (25mm) wash brush
- no. 0 (old), no. 4 and no. 8 flats
- 10/0 Dressden liner
- no. 2 filbert (cat's tongue)
- 10/0 round
- ⅛-inch (3mm) angle
- ¼-inch (6mm) flat comb (rake)

COLOR PALETTE

Ceramcoat Antique White

FolkArt Buttercup

FolkArt Fresh Foliage

FolkArt Coastal Blue

Ceramcoat Mudstone

Accent Crown Jewels Imperial Antique Gold

Ceramcoat Lavender

Americana Red Violet

Americana Blue Haze

Americana Asphaltum

Americana Hauser Dark Green

Ceramcoat Dark Night Blue

FolkArt Metallics Sequin Black

3 Prepare the wood following the basic prep instructions on page 14. If your compact has a film on it, clean it with an alcohol wipe, then a damp rag. Do this after you sand and before you seal. Test to see how well the compact opens and closes; sanding it a little may help it open and close more easily.
4 Spray with two thin coats of Black Krylon Satin. Allow to dry.
5 Remove the tape from the edges. Use a permanent black marker to color these. (I've found this is the best way to eliminate paint buildup.)

The Scene

This is a very simple scene. It can be done very quickly if you don't get caught up in perfecting the detail. Since it's so small and part of the background, if you try to make it more detailed, it gets confusing.

SCENE PATTERN OUTLINE
Transfer this pattern onto surface.

SCENE DETAILED DESIGN
Use for reference; don't transfer these lines.

SCENE BORDER PATTERN OUTLINE
Transfer this pattern.

PATTERN FOR SIDE OF COMPACT
Transfer this pattern.

TOP OF COMPACT DETAILED DESIGN
Use for reference; don't transfer these lines.

BACK OF COMPACT DETAILED DESIGN
Transfer only the basic outline.

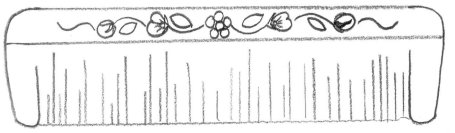

COMB PATTERN

PATTERN FOR INSIDE OF COMPACT

The patterns and designs on this page may be hand-traced or photocopied for personal use only. Shown at full size.

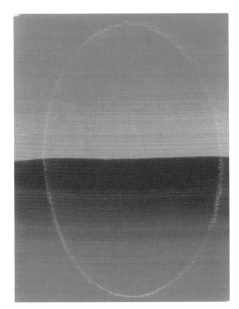

1 *The Scene*

So you don't have to worry about going outside the oval as you paint the scene, we will paint the scene first, then go back and "frame" the oval later. Open the compact while painting the top. Moisten your wash brush with flow medium and double load with Coastal Blue and Lavender. Blend, then stroke over the top half of the oval with the blue side to the top as shown. You won't see much of this once the scene and oval are complete. This just gives the scene a base and keeps the perspective clear. Keep this application as flat and smooth as possible or you'll see ridges in the finished scene. Rinse the brush, moisten with flow medium and double load with Blue Haze and Coastal Blue. Stroke over the bottom half with the Coastal Blue side of the brush to the bottom of the scene. Allow to dry. Trace the oval pattern from page 58, cut out and center over the scene area. Lightly trace the oval over the base colors with a chalk pencil.

2

Trace the scene pattern outline onto tracing paper and trim away excess paper. Use the chalk method (page 15) to transfer the pattern lightly with a stylus. Refer to the guide on page 60 for help in painting the elements. For the clouds, moisten a no. 2 filbert with flow medium, then double load with Antique White plus Blue Haze. This will look rather dramatic until you add the leaves. Try to avoid creating texture in the paint. Add a little highlight with a wash of Buttercup (1). Double load a no. 2 filbert, moistened with flow medium, with Buttercup and Lavender. Blend and brush in the hills (2). For the background trees, moisten a ¼-inch (6mm) or ⅛-inch (3mm) comb with flow medium and dip the tip in a thinned mix of Blue Haze plus a touch of Antique White. Stroke on the palette until the hairs separate—this won't work if the paint is too thick. Pull the background trees. You can also use a 10/0 round to stroke little lines across the background (3). Make a little haze in front of the tree line with a no. 2 filbert and Hauser Dark Green plus a touch of Antique White thinned with flow medium (4). Base the foreground grass with a no. 2 filbert and Hauser Dark Green (5). Add the tree trunk with a 10/0 round and thinned Asphaltum. Keep the branches delicate (6). Add a shadow of the foreground shore in the water with a 10/0 round and Dark Night Blue (7).

3 Stipple the shaded leaves with thinned Dark Night Blue and an old or scruffy no. 0 flat brush, using a light pouncing motion (1). Add trunk shadows with a 10/0 round and thinned Dark Night Blue (2). Mix half Fresh Foliage and half Buttercup and thin a little, then use a comber or 10/0 round to highlight the grass (3).

4 Stipple more leaves with an old no. 0 flat and Hauser Dark Green with a little Fresh Foliage, as shown (1). Add to the grass with the comb and drybrush a little with a no. 2 filbert (2).

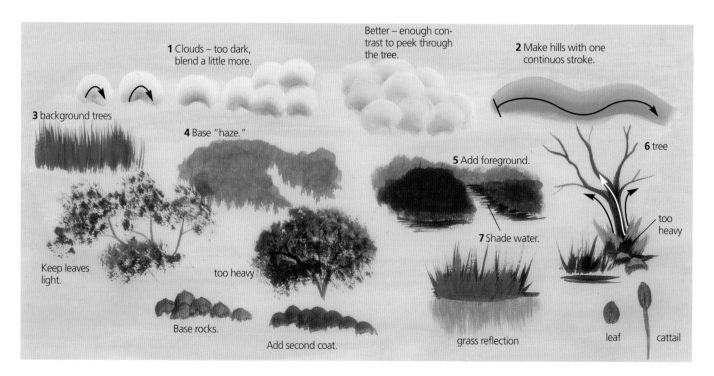

1 Clouds – too dark, blend a little more.

Better – enough contrast to peek through the tree.

2 Make hills with one continuos stroke.

3 background trees

4 Base "haze."

5 Add foreground.

6 tree

too heavy

Keep leaves light.

too heavy

7 Shade water.

Base rocks.

Add second coat.

grass reflection

leaf

cattail

5 Stipple Fresh Foliage on the tree with an old no. 0 flat (1). Use a comb or 10/0 round and thinned Dark Night Blue to add the shore base (2). Use Asphaltum and a no. 2 filbert to touch in the rocks (3). Tap a medium highlight on the rocks with a no. 2 filbert and Asphaltum + a little Antique White (4). Add Dark Night Blue shadows to the water with a 10/0 round; add a few highlights with Coastal Blue (5). Add grass with a 10/0 liner using Dark Night Blue, then Hauser Dark Green. Paint in some cattails using Asphaltum (6).

6 Use Buttercup to add a few brighter highlights to the Fresh Foliage areas (1). Tip the bristles of a no. 2 filbert in Mudstone and dab a little on the rocks for highlights (2). Add highlights to the tree and cattails using a 10/0 round and Asphaltum + a little Buttercup (3). Dry completely. Brush J.W. etc. Right-Step Satin Varnish over the scene. Dry for a minimum of twenty-four hours.

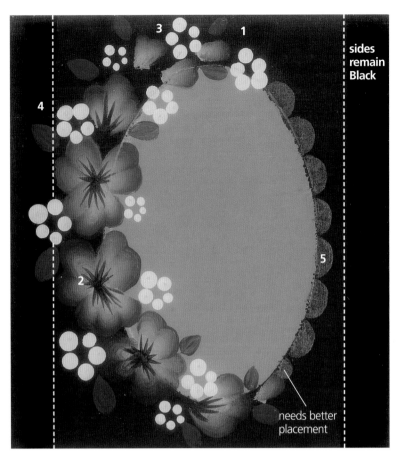

sides
remain
Black

needs better
placement

7 Framing the Picture

After the scene is thoroughly dry, it's time to put the frame on. Trace the oval outline onto contact paper and cut it out. Remove the backing and press the contact paper oval over the scene to protect it. Blend Dark Night Blue onto a no. 8 flat moistened with a little flow medium. With the compact open, apply two to three coats to the top of the compact (1). When dry, remove the contact paper. Double load an ⅛-inch (3mm) angle with Red Violet on the top half and Buttercup on the bottom half. Blend, then follow the instructions on page 63 to paint the pansies and add the middle veins (2). Next add the dot flowers with a stylus and Antique White; make five petals. I've made two sizes of dot flowers. You can vary the sizes or do them all the same. You don't want them to take over (3). Add leaves with a mix of half Fresh Foliage and half Hauser Dark Green (see page 63). Use 10/0 round to add the stems (4). Dip a no. 2 filbert in Imperial Antique Gold and start with the middle scallop on the right border of the oval (5). Next put one at the top of the right side and one at the bottom. Evenly divide the areas between into scallops.

8

Add dots to center of the pansies with a stylus and Buttercup. Add Coastal Blue dots to the centers of the small white flowers. Highlight the pansies and leaves using a 10/0 round and Imperial Antique Gold (1). Also go all along the edges of the top using small, tapped strokes (2). With a 10/0 liner add an edge to the oval scene with thinned Dark Night Blue (3). With a stylus, add thinned Dark Night Blue dots to the scallops (4).

Place the brush at an angle with Red Violet to the top. Pivot only the top of the brush.

Make a small bud the same way. Stop in the middle and add another petal.

For an open bud, repeat to add another petal.

Use a 10/0 round with thinned Dark Night Blue to paint the middle veins. Start from center and work out.

Keep the bottom of the brush in the middle for a full pansy.

Use half Fresh Foliage and half Hauser Dark Green on a 10/0 round to make two strokes for leaves. You can combine them or keep them split to create a vein line.

Add a Lavender highlight with two strokes of a 10/0 round.

9 Finishing Touches

Now that the top is finished, you should be able to add the finishing touches with ease. With 3M Long-Mask Masking Tape, tape off the square on the back. Brush sealer over the back and allow to dry. This will keep paint from bleeding under the tape. Give the back two basecoats of Dark Night Blue with a no. 8 flat. Allow to dry, but leave the tape on. Following the back pattern, paint the flowers. Using a 10/0 round and Imperial Antique Gold, add highlights, then add the scalloped edges on the inside of the tape. When dry, take off the tape. Use a no. 4 flat with Sequin Black to go over the sides, back side and inside. This adds a nice

touch—the paint has tiny gold sparkles in it. Follow the side pattern for the pansies. Finish off the inside with a 10/0 round and Imperial Antique Gold, making little "taps" around the mirror and strokes in the corners. I used a no. 2 filbert with Imperial Antique Gold to make three strokes together, joining at the ends. I overstroked these with Dark Night Blue on a 10/0 round. When the entire compact is finished, dry overnight and apply J.W. etc. Right-Step Satin Varnish. To finish the comb, just follow the pattern. When dry, varnish and let dry one hour, then peel off the blue tape. Add a little Imperial Antique Gold border where the tape was and your comb is completed.

Hat Pin Box and Jewelry Set

*I*t's always an adventure when looking for a new way to paint a background. I set out one day to find plain window screen for another project. When I saw the Gutter Guard used in this project, I was struck with ideas! I could hardly wait to see the results when the paint went through the mesh—and sure enough, the possibilities were endless.

The top of the box has an enameled look, similar to a compact that was my Gramzy's. The earrings and brooch are painted to match and add to the charm when stored inside.

Preparation

Follow the directions for basic wood preparation in chapter three to prepare all of the pieces. We'll work on the box first. The inside bottom of the box is flocked, so you don't need to prepare it.

ENLARGED DESIGN FOR EARRING FLOWERS

EARRING PATTERN
Transfer this pattern to surface.

SURFACES

- 2¼" × 5¼" (5.7cm × 13.3cm) wooden hat pin box
- wooden button earrings
- 1⅝-inch (4.1cm) wooden button
- pin and earring backs

ADDITIONS TO BASIC SUPPLIES

- Bond 527 Multi-Purpose Cement or other strong glue
- Amerimax Gutter Guard plastic mesh (check hardware stores)
- razor blade

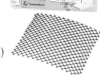

BRUSHES

- ¾-inch (19mm) wash brush
- no. 0, no. 2, no. 4, no. 6 and no. 12 flats
- 10/0 Dressden liner
- mini filbert (cat's tongue)
- 10/0 round
- no. 0 Kolinsky red sable round
- old no. 2 flat
- no. 12 ox hair pouncer or ¾-inch (19mm) round stencil brush
- old no. 4 filbert (for speckle brush)

COLOR PALETTE

Ceramcoat Gleams Pearl Finish	Americana White Wash	Jo Sonja's Silver	DecoArt Dazzling Metallics Champagne Gold	Jo Sonja's Pale Gold
Jo Sonja's Rich Gold	Ceramcoat Gleams Bronze	FolkArt Metallics Rose Shimmer	FolkArt Metallics Plum	Accent Crown Jewels Crown Red Velvet
FolkArt Metallics Peridot	Ceramcoat Mallard Green	Accent Classical Bronze	FolkArt Metallics Sequin Black	Ceramcoat Black

ENLARGED DESIGN FOR BROOCH FLOWER

BROOCH PATTERN
Transfer this pattern to surface. All patterns on this page are full size.

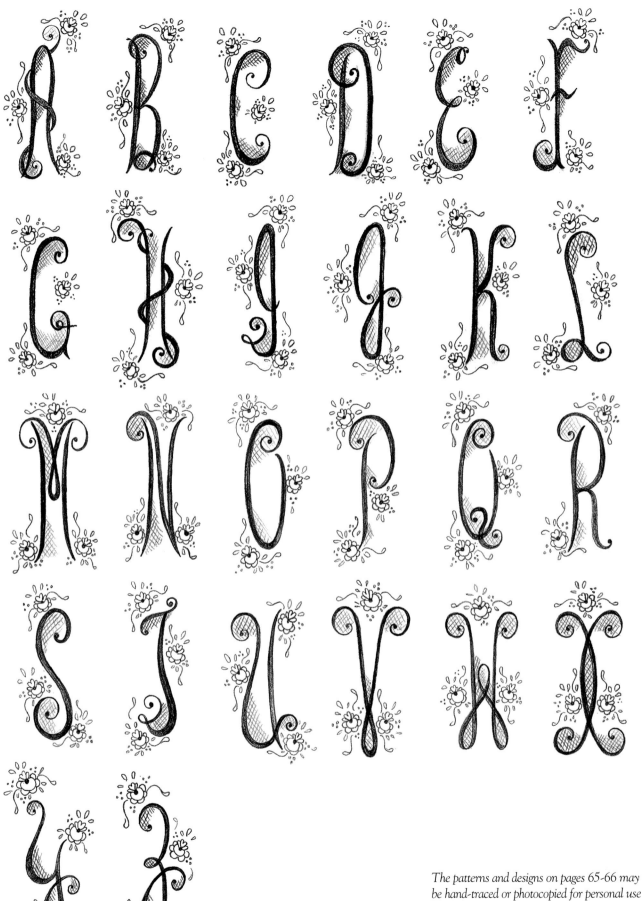

The patterns and designs on pages 65-66 may be hand-traced or photocopied for personal use only. Enlarge the initial of your choice at 182% to return to full size and transfer to the top of your box.

Bottom and Sides of Box

1 Give the bottom and sides two coats of Classical Bronze mixed with a little flow medium. Use a ¾-inch (19mm) wash brush. Allow to dry (1). Cut the Gutter Guard into five pieces, one for each side and the bottom. Dip a pouncer or stencil brush in a puddle of Bronze and work the paint halfway up the bristles, then blot off on napkins. You want to have enough paint in the bristles to leave color when you pounce through the mesh, but you don't want to blob it on. Make sure the mesh is straight and centered, then pounce Bronze lightly through the holes (2). Match each side with the pattern on the previous one. Allow to dry.

2 Use a no. 2 flat and Champagne Gold to make little diamonds in the top portion of each Bronze diamond. Work in diagonal rows (3). Using a 10/0 round, paint Pale Gold strokes along the top edge of each horizontal row (4).

3 Flip the box over and paint Pale Gold strokes along the other edge of each horizontal row (5). Using a 10/0 round and Silver, make little comma strokes in the middle of each **X** formed by the Pale Gold strokes. Work in a diagonal (6). The following steps are shown completed on page 64. When dry, add a little highlight to the side edges. Dip an old no. 2 flat in Champagne Gold and work the paint in until you achieve drybrush consistency. Rub the brush over all of the side edges. Allow to dry. Apply a hint of Bronze mixed with Kleister to the entire box using a ¾-inch (19mm) wash. Use no. 6 and no. 4 flats to give the rim and inside of the box two coats of the Bronze mix. Let the Classical Bronze show through a little. Allow to dry. Varnish with Jo Sonja's Gloss Varnish. Allow to cure twenty-four hours. Wax if desired. Apply black flock to the inside bottom, following the instructions on the package.

4 The Lid

Use thin, transparent painter's tape to tape around the edges. Apply J.W. etc. First Step Wood Sealer to the middle of the lid. Apply three coats of White Wash with a no. 12 flat, drying to the touch between coats. Apply two coats of Pearl Finish over the white with the no. 12 flat. Trace the initial of your choice onto tracing paper and transfer using the CPC method (page 15). Break your initial into strokes, using the **E** shown here as an example. Load a no. 0 round with Black thinned with a little water. Start at the top of your letter and join the strokes. Overstroke with Sequin Black.

clear tape

5

The rose is very simple to do—just follow the steps shown above using a mini filbert and Rose Shimmer. Use a 10/0 round and Plum to make the lavender flowers. Use a 10/0 round and Peridot to make the leaves and Classical Bronze for the stems. Add the Rich Gold strokes and dots using a 10/0 round and a stylus (see finished design above.)

6 When your design is finished and dry, apply Jo Sonja's Crackle Medium with a no. 12 flat. Crackle medium should be applied no more than two hours after the surface is dry for best results. When the crackle medium is dry, make an antiquing mixture of Pearl Finish plus a touch of Sequin Black and thin with retarder so the mixture can seep into the cracks. Apply to the lid and wipe over immediately with a soft cloth (1). Next, make a "speckle" brush by cutting an old no. 4 filbert with a razor blade as shown below. Use a slightly darker version of the antiquing mix to apply age speckles around the edge of the design—lightly dip the tips in the mixture and "tap" where needed (2). Remove the tape carefully. Using a no. 6 flat, follow the edge of the "porcelain" area with Classical Bronze, paint the sides and back of the lid with two to three coats of the same color on a no. 12 flat. Allow to dry (3). Using a 10/0 liner and Rich Gold thinned with flow medium, paint rows of lines around the top (4) and along the side edges. With a 10/0 liner and Silver thinned with flow medium, paint a border line all around the top (5). Using a stylus and Pale Gold, add dots over the Silver line (6). When the lid is completely dry, brush over it lightly with a glaze made of Kleister plus a touch of Bronze. Allow to dry overnight, then apply Jo Sonja's Gloss Varnish. If desired, wax after curing for twenty-four hours.

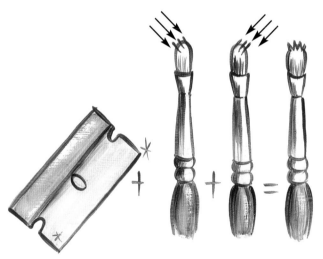

making a "speckle" brush

White Wash +
touch Rose
Shimmer

half White Wash +
half Rose Shimmer

Plum + Rose
Shimmer

Crown Red Velvet
+ touch Black

Plum + touch Black

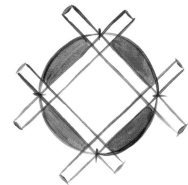

taping the brooch

adding the white square

Brooch Flowers

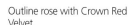

Outline rose with Crown Red Velvet.

Fill center in with Crown Red Velvet and add stroke to bud. Fill the petals in and paint bud with Rose Shimmer.

Give center second coat of Crown Red Velvet. Add Rose Shimmer + Plum to outer petals. Add Black to rose center. Add Plum to the lavender flowers. Paint leaves with a mini filbert double loaded with Peridot and Crown Red Velvet.

Use half White Wash + half Rose Shimmer to paint the top petal, highlight the outer petals and stroke the inner petals. Add Peridot leaves and bud stems.

Highlight with White Wash + a touch of Rose Shimmer. Add the bowl line with Crown Red Velvet + a touch of Black. Strengthen the outer petals with Crown Red Velvet. Add Classical Bronze details for the stems. Add Rich Gold dots.

7 Brooch and Earring Set

Base with two to three coats of Black. Dry completely. Divide the brooch into four equal sections and lay the tape across the brooch evenly, leaving the ends long enough to tape the brooch down to a clipboard or piece of cardboard. This will help keep the brooch in place as well as mask off the center square. You will stroke the square onto the earrings freehand—they're too small to tape off. Roll a piece of 3M Long-Mask Masking Tape sticky side up in paper chain fashion. Use this to tape the earrings down on the same board as the brooch. If the blue tape lets go too easily, try clear mailing tape—just be careful not to pull the paint off. Apply three coats of White Wash and two coats of Pearl Finish to the brooch and earrings with a no. 4 flat. I've enlarged the flowers so you can see more easily how they're created. You can trace the flowers on the brooch using the CPC method (see page 15) or paint them freehand. Follow the steps at left to paint the flowers using a 10/0 round and a mini filbert. When you've finished the flowers, brush crackle medium over them. When dry, brush the antique mix on and wipe off. Add a few age speckles. If you want a quicker version, you could just sponge the antique mixture on top of the White Wash and Pearl Finish, then paint the flowers on. Carefully remove the tape from the brooch, then secure it to the board with a tape loop as you did the earrings.

Earring Flowers

Outline with Crown Red Velvet

Fill in with Rose Shimmer. Add Black dot to center.

Lighten inner petals with half White Wash + half Rose Shimmer. Add Peridot leaves.

Highlight with White Wash + a touch of Rose Shimmer. Add Classical Bronze veins. Add Rich Gold dots.

8 Finishing the Brooch

Using a no. 4 flat and Mallard Green, paint along the edges of the white square on the brooch as shown (1). Use a 10/0 liner with thinned Rich Gold to make three even, diagonal lines on top of each Mallard Green area (2). Add two more lines between the first three (3). Cross these lines with diagonals going the other way (4), then add short lines to fill in the ends (5). See the illustration below for help in painting the gold lines. Now paint even rows of lines on the black area with Rich Gold and a 10/0 liner (6). Add more lines between the first lines (7). Continue to add lines between the previous lines (8), then add two border lines on either side of the Mallard Green areas (9). Add a Rich Gold dot at each corner of the white square (10). Add three Rich Gold strokes above the dots with a 10/0 liner (11). Add Pale Gold overstrokes over the previous three strokes (12).

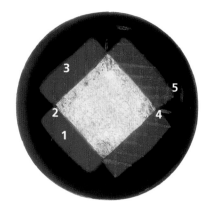

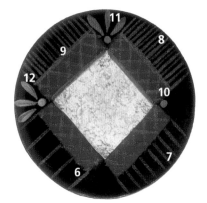

When painting the gold lines, think of the lines as continuous vertical lines.

Think of continuous horizontal lines when painting the crossing lines. You can turn the brooch or earrings so you're actually pulling these lines vertically if you find it easier to work that way.

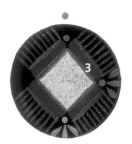

9 Finishing the Earrings

Add Mallard Green to the earrings using a no. 0 flat (1). Use a 10/0 round to add the lines over the black area as you did for the brooch (2). Add the same finishing touches to the earrings as you did the brooch, using a 10/0 round (3). The final touch is to brush a gold shimmer over the earrings and brooch with Kleister plus a touch of Rich Gold. The best way to varnish these pieces is with Krylon Crystal Clear Acrylic Spray, no. 1303A. When dry, use strong glue to fasten on the backs.

Victorian Vanity Box and Mirror

The Victorian era is one of the most beautiful fashion periods in history. Everything from simple tools to clothes to homes were ornately decked out. You can add these ornate touches to your own furnishings and accessories with nothing more than a brush and paint—just another aspect of what makes decorative painting so exciting!

This Victorian lady might be a little overdone for your taste, but sometimes it's hard to stop! You don't have to add all the feathers and makeup; she can easily be made less ornate. However you design her, I hope she will be a delight to look upon as well as to paint.

Preparing the Surfaces

It probably seems funny to turn a Nordic bowl into a Victorian box, but that's what we're going to do. This box is pretty versatile, so we can get away with it.

1 Cut the contact paper down to fit over the mirror. Remove the back from the contact paper and stick it to the mirror. Use the razor blade to trim it to fit. This will protect the mirror from sanding dust and paint.

2 Follow the basic wood preparation instructions in chapter three to prepare the box and mirror back.

3 We're going to create an abalone look for the top of the box. It may look difficult, but it's very simple and fast to do. If you mess up, you can easily remove the paint. We'll be working wet-on-wet, so it should take only about ten minutes to complete the lid.

MATERIALS

SURFACES
- 4-inch diameter (10.2cm) Nordic bowl
- 2½-inch (6.4cm) purse mirror

ADDITIONS TO BASIC SUPPLIES
- small piece of contact paper
- razor blade
- two soft, clean cloths

BRUSHES
- ¾-inch (19mm) wash brush
- no. 0, no. 2, no. 4, no. 6, no. 8 and no. 10 flats
- no. 2 and mini filberts (cat's tongues)
- 10/0 Dressden liner
- 10/0 round
- old no. 2 filbert
- a few old brushes for gold leafing and flocking
- medium mop or Suzie's Pit-I-Pat brush

COLOR PALETTE

DecoArt Dazzling Metallics Oyster Pearl

Jo Sonja's Blue Iridescent

Jo Sonja's Green Iridescent

Jo Sonja's Violet Iridescent

Jo Sonja's Red Iridescent

Jo Sonja's Warm White

Jo Sonja's Opal

Jo Sonja's Skin Tone Base

Jo Sonja's Jaune Brillant

Jo Sonja's Moss Green

Jo Sonja's Rich Gold

Jo Sonja's Provincial Beige

Jo Sonja's Permanent Alizarine

Jo Sonja's Olive Green

Jo Sonja's Pthalo Green

Jo Sonja's Dioxazine Purple

Jo Sonja's Purple Madder

Jo Sonja's Burnt Umber

Jo Sonja's Payne's Grey

Jo Sonja's Carbon Black

Jo Sonja's Victorian Red

**PATTERN OUTLINE
FOR BOX**

**DETAILED DESIGN
FOR BOX**

**PATTERN FOR
BACK OF MIRROR**

*These patterns and designs may be hand-
traced or photocopied for personal use only.
Shown at full size.*

**PATTERN FOR
SIDE OF BOX**

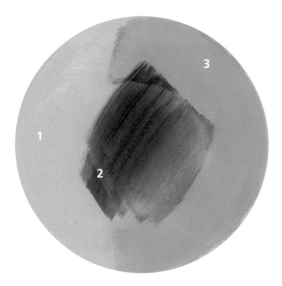

1 Base the top of the box lid with two coats of Opal mixed with a touch of flow medium on a ¾-inch (19mm) wash brush (1). Dry between coats. (Don't worry about the edges, you'll gold leaf them later.) When dry, rub a thin coat of retarder over the Opal paint. Using a no. 10 flat, brush Payne's Grey over the middle (2). Working quickly, rinse the brush and apply Moss Green around the entire edge and up to the Payne's Grey while it is still wet (3).

2 Continue to work wet-on-wet. Dip a no. 10 flat in retarder, dab off on a napkin, then dip into Purple Madder. Brush diagonal strokes of Purple Madder around the edges of the Payne's Grey area (1). Rinse the brush, dip in retarder, dab off, then load with Warm White. Make more diagonal strokes, tapering off as you go toward the center. Don't be too perfect, add some slightly crooked lines for character (2).

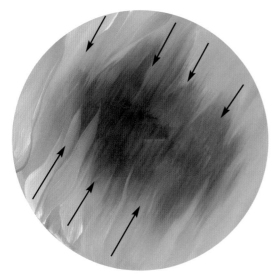

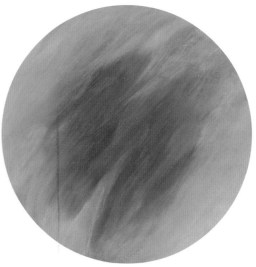

3 Blend at a diagonal, allowing streaks and colors to show definition. Use a dry medium mop brush to soften. Don't overblend or it will become muddy. If you aren't happy with the effect, put some retarder on a rag and wipe the paint off—only the opal base should remain—and you can start over. Allow to dry overnight. (At this time you could skip to page 76 and work on the bottom of the box and the mirror.)

4 When step three is dry, use a no. 10 flat to randomly glaze Oyster Peal, Blue Iridescent, Green Iridescent, Violet Iridescent and Red Iridescent over the lid, using a little flow medium to keep the colors smooth and transparent. Allow to dry at least three hours—overnight is best—then spray with Krylon Matte Finish Spray, no. 1311. Mix Victorian Red + a touch of Pthalo Green and basecoat the bottom and sides of the lid with two coats of this mix.

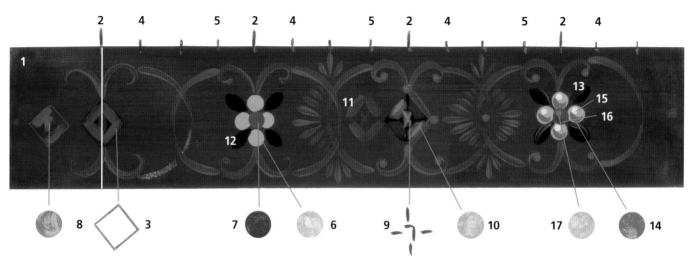

5 The Box And Mirror

Paint the inside of the box Carbon Black (later to be flocked). Use a ¾-inch (19mm) wash brush and a no. 10 flat to paint the rim and outside of the box and mirror with two coats of the Victorian Red/Pthalo Green mix from step four—add a little flow medium (1). You can try to transfer the design on using tracing paper and chalk but it may come out off-center due to the slope of the sides. I've found it's best to mark the box off and use circle and square templates to put the design on. Use white chalk to divide the top of the rim in half (shown at right). Next divide the rim into fourths, then eighths, marking each division. Divide each eighth in half to come up with sixteen equal divisions. Now divide each sixteenth in half; your rim is now divided into thirty-two equal areas. Now that you have some guidelines, it will be easy to lay out the design. At each eighth mark, draw a line straight down the side with chalk (2). Halfway down every other line you just drew, create a small diamond (use a square template tilted so one corner points up) with a chalk pencil (3). Place the center of a 1⅛-inch (2.9cm) circle template so it lines up with the ½ mark to the right of the first diamond you drew. Lightly trace inside the right half of the template with a chalk pencil (4). Repeat on each ½ mark to the right of the eighth lines. Then go back around the box lining up the center point of the template with the ½ lines to the left of each eighth line and tracing the left half of the circle. It will overlap the end of the first

(5). Using a no. 8 flat and Pthalo Green, fill in the diamonds with one stroke. Paint pearls on every other eighth line using an EZ Dotz tool or the end of a brush handle and a mix of Oyster Pearl plus Burnt Umber thinned with flow medium; this shouldn't be runny (6). Repeat for the pearl centers using a mix of Warm White plus a little Dioxazine Purple (7). Use a 10/0 liner and Rich Gold thinned with a little flow medium to paint the stroke-work as shown. It's best to paint the same stroke all the way around the box rather than complete one segment at a time. Don't add the gold dots until the gems are finished. Add the medium-value details to the diamonds with Pthalo Green plus a touch of Warm White on a no. 2 flat (8). Add the Carbon Black details to the diamonds using a 10/0 round (9). Add the light value with Warm White plus a touch of Pthalo Green (10). Finish with a highlight of Green Iridescent (11). Add Pthalo Green leaves to the pearl clusters using a mini filbert (12). Highlight the leaves with Green Iridescent (13). Add shadows to the pearls with Opal plus a touch of Carbon Black on a 10/0 round (14). Highlight the pearls with Warm White on a stylus (15). Add shadows to the center pearls with Dioxazine Purple and a 10/0 round (16), then highlight with Warm White plus a touch of Dioxazine Purple on a stylus (17). Add the gold dots with Rich Gold thinned with flow medium. Use the chalk method to transfer the design to the mirror, dust off and paint as directed above.

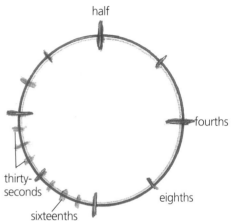

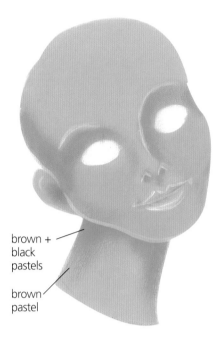

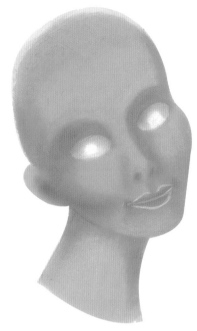

brown +
black
pastels

brown
pastel

6 The Victorian Lady

If you're not ready to paint a face, you could paint the mirror motif on the lid instead. Copy the basic outline of the lady onto tracing paper. Use Super Chacopaper to trace only the head and neck onto the lid. Use a no. 8 or no. 6 flat (the bigger the brush the smoother the basecoat) to base the head and neck with Warm White and a little flow medium (not shown). This will block out the background and provide a better base. Dry. Cut a 3M Sanding Sponge into a small square and lightly sand over the Warm White. Use a no. 6 flat and Skin Tone Base plus a touch of Jaune Brillant and a little flow medium to paint over the Warm White base. Keep your strokes smooth. Apply two to three coats, drying well and sanding lightly between. Use the white chalk method (page 15) to trace only the face and neck lines on. Dust off. Paint in the eye background with a mini filbert and Warm White. Apply two to three coats. Rub a brown chalk pastel on sandpaper to create dust. Repeat with a black pastel. You don't need much. Dip an old, dry filbert into the brown dust first and shade the face and neck as shown. Then mix a touch of black dust with the brown to deepen the shading.

7

Continue to strengthen the shadows, adding a little pink pastel dust for the cheeks. The white chalk lines will disappear as you work. Don't rinse the brush or get it wet—remove unwanted color by rubbing the brush between your fingers, then dip into the next color. If you aren't happy with the shading, remove it with a damp Q-tip. This may make it hard to reblend an area and you may have to start over with the shading. Once you're satisfied with the color, use a small dry mop brush to dust it off, then spray with Krylon Matte Finish Spray, no. 1311. This will make the shading permanent.

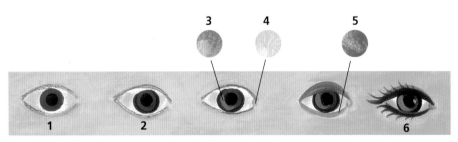

8

I've outlined the base of the eye so you can see it better—don't outline yours yet. Use a mini filbert and Olive Green to add the iris, then add a Carbon Black pupil with a large stylus or EZ Dotz tool (1). Outline the iris with Pthalo Green on a 10/0 round, leaving the top open (2). Use a 10/0 round to add Warm White plus a touch of Olive Green to the eye (3). Add a dot of Warm White plus a touch of Permanent Alizarine for the tear duct (4). Paint the upper eyelid with Provincial Beige. Paint the lower eyelid with Warm White plus a touch of Burnt Umber (5). Use Burnt Umber and a 10/0 round for the eyeliner and lashes. Add a Green Iridescent highlight to the iris with a 10/0 round (6).

9 Use Provincial Beige and a 10/0 round to paint the nose (1) and eyebrows (2). Deepen the eyebrow color with a mix of Provincial Beige and Burnt Umber (3). Stroke in the mouth with a no. 0 flat and a mix of Warm White plus Permanent Alizarine. Use a 10/0 round and Provincial Beige for the detail lines (4). Use a darker mix of Permanent Alizarine plus Warm White and a 10/0 round to outline the lips (5). Highlight the lips with a lighter mix of Permanent Alizarine and Warm White on a 10/0 round (6). Finish by detailing the lips with Permanent Alizarine plus a touch of Burnt Umber (7).

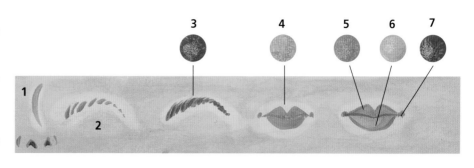

10 At this point your lady's face should be completed. I've left the features on this face a little less refined; you can paint yours like this if you prefer a more toned-down look. Trace the rest of the basic design onto the surface with Super Chacopaper. Paint the hair and feathers with Burnt Umber on a no. 2 flat, following the detail at left (1). Base in the blouse and collar with Olive Green and a touch of Warm White on a no. 4 flat (2). Base in the tie with Warm White on a no. 4 flat; mix in a little Olive Green for the bottom half (3). With Permanent Alizarine, base the upper hat veil and large feather using a no. 4 flat and the top feathers with a no. 0 flat (4). Base the sleeves with a no. 8 flat and Victorian Red (5). Using Olive Green plus Warm White, add the hatband using a no. 0 flat and the collar using a no. 4 flat (6). Use a 10/0 round to add hair and feather detail with Carbon Black (7). Swirl in more feather detail with a no. 2 filbert and Dioxazine Purple (8). When the hair is dry, add the veil with a no. 4 flat and Green Iridescent thinned with flow medium. Add folds using a no. 2 flat double loaded with Olive Green and Green Iridescent thinned with a little flow medium and blended well (9). Add the gem with a no. 2 flat and Pthalo Green plus a touch of Warm White (10). Brush shadows into the upper veil in a zigzag fashion, using a no. 4 flat double loaded with Burnt Umber and Permanent Alizarine (11). Detail the ear with a 10/0 round and Provincial Beige (12). Base the earring with Opal plus a touch of Carbon Black on a 10/0 round (13). Shade the sleeves with Victorian Red plus a touch of Burnt Umber on a no. 4 flat (14). Highlight the sleeves with Victorian Red and a touch of Warm White (15). Use a 10/0 round and Burnt Umber to add swirl details to the blouse (16). With Warm White and a 10/0 round, add scallops to the tie (17).

11 Add medium highlights to the hair with Provincial Beige and a 10/0 round (1). Add light to the hair and long feathers with Rich Gold on a 10/0 round (2). Using a 10/0 round, detail the feathers working dark to light with Dioxazine Purple, Dioxazine Purple plus a touch of Warm White, Warm White plus a touch of Dioxazine Purple and then Violet Iridescent (3). Give the collar a sheer look using Warm White and a touch of Olive Green with a 10/0 round to add a few streaks, eyelet dots and small ruffles (4). Using Provincial Beige and Warm White on a 10/0 round, outline the scallops on the tie and add dots and flower centers. Add highlights to the collar and tie with Oyster Pearl and Warm White on a 10/0 round (5). With Victorian Red and a touch of Burnt Umber, add details to sleeve with a 10/0 round (6). Paint the tie clip with Rich Gold, then Carbon Black on a 10/0 round and add a little Green Iridescent to the center (7). Use a 10/0 round to base the collar rim with Burnt Umber, then add Green Iridescent highlights (8). Add light pink highlight strokes to the veil with a 10/0 round and Warm White plus a touch of Permanent Alizarine (9). Mix Green Iridescent with a touch of Warm White plus Olive Green and add crisscross strokes to the veil using a 10/0 round (10). Mix Violet Iridescent with a touch of Pthalo Green plus Warm White and add middle veins to the small feathers. Highlight these feathers with a 10/0 round and Blue Iridescent (11). Finish the hat brooch using a 10/0 round and Carbon Black to add eyebrow strokes on the outer edge of the gem, and line details to the gem. Go back over the eyebrow strokes with Rich Gold. Add various values of Pthalo Green plus Warm White to the gem (12). Using Provincial Beige and a touch of Burnt Umber, define the chin and neck a little more with a 10/0 round (13). Finish the earring (detail shown at the bottom of the illustration) using a stylus dipped in Opal. Next dip a smaller stylus in Warm White for the highlight, then Permanent Alizarine for the center. Add leaves to the earring with a 10/0 round and Pthalo Green (14).

12 *Finishing the Box*
After the lid has had a chance to dry, remove any Chaco lines with a damp Q-tip, then use a damp white cloth to wipe the top lightly to pick up dust. Spray with Krylon Crystal Clear Acrylic Spray, no. 1303A. Follow the directions on your package of gold leaf to gold leaf the edges and bottom of the lid and the bottom of the box. You can give it a solid gold look or let cracks of the background color show through. If the gold is too bright, you can antique it. Varnish the gold leaf when you're finished. I used Krylon Crystal Clear Acrylic Spray since I'd already used it on this piece. Follow the directions on the flocking package to apply black flocking over the black base inside the bowl. When you apply the flock, it's best to do it over a large sheet of paper. The flock is "blown" out of the tube. Leave it to sit overnight; when dry, tap the excess flock out onto the paper and pour back into the bottle. This completes our box and mirror. I hope you learned something new!

Switch Plate and Mini Clock

You may have guessed by now that I'm fond of antiques. About seven years ago we bought an old farm (or "dump," as my husband would say). What I saw were the beautiful glass doorknobs, an old hutch, wooden floors—and that's about all we saved! It was a lot of work to make the house livable again, but I'm thankful my husband and others didn't give up.

It's been fun adding more "junk" to the "dump." We have a little sitting room that needed a better switch plate and this is what I came up with. It needed something to go with it and a clock is always useful.

You can easily change the colors to suit your decor. Don't be scared off by all the strokework. When you break it down into sections it goes very fast.

MATERIALS

SURFACES
- double switch plate
- mini clock

ADDITIONS TO BASIC SUPPLIES
- piece of vinyl window screen

- small piece of Styrofoam
- four fancy tacks or screws
- clean, soft cloth

BRUSHES
- ¾-inch (19mm) wash brush
- no. 4, no. 6 and no. 8 flats
- no. 2 and mini filberts (cat's tongues)
- 10/0 Dressden liner
- 10/0 round

COLOR PALETTE

Jo Sonja's Rich Gold | Jo Sonja's Background Color Vellum | Jo Sonja's Provincial Beige | Jo Sonja's Antique Green | Jo Sonja's Red Violet

Preparing the Surfaces

1 Prepare the switch plate and clock as described on page 14 in basic wood prep.

2 Basecoat the entire switch plate and clock with Antique Green mixed with a little flow medium, using a ¾-inch (19mm) wash brush. Apply one coat, dry, then use a 3M Sanding Sponge to lightly smooth the paint. Apply a second coat and allow to dry.

3 Some people don't mind leaving the back of the switch plate bare, but I like to finish mine. It just seems tacky to make the top look nice, then flip it over to bare wood with dribbles of paint. It takes away from the craftsmanship of the piece. To finish the back of the switch plate, paint the switch holes with Red Violet using a no. 4 flat. When you finish, wipe away any excess Red Violet on the front. When dry, rub the back with a little retarder. Moisten a ¾-inch (19mm) wash brush with retarder, dab off, then double load with Red Violet and Rich Gold. Starting at the top left, hold the brush straight up on the bristles and lightly stroke downward. Work across the plate in 1-inch (2.5cm) rows, always overlapping the previous row. You'll be surprised at how fast you can do this. When you're done, let dry overnight, then spray with Krylon Crystal Clear Acrylic Spray, no. 1303A. You can work on the clock while you're waiting for the switch plate to dry.

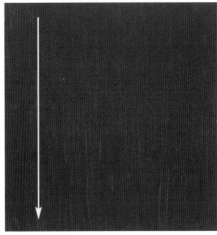

Stroke downward with a double-loaded brush to finish the back of the switch plate.

BASIC PATTERN OUTLINE FOR SWITCH PLATE
Transfer this design onto surface.

DETAILED DESIGN FOR SWITCH PLATE

The patterns and designs on pages 82-83 may be hand-traced or photocopied for personal use only. Enlarge at 133% to return to full size.

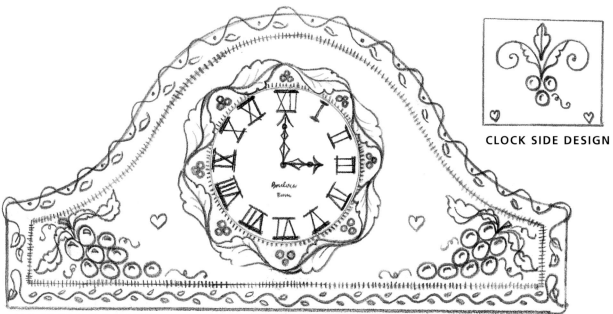

CLOCK SIDE DESIGN

CLOCK FRONT DESIGN

CLOCK BACK DESIGN

CLOCK TOP DESIGN

1 The Clock Front

Using a no. 6 or no. 8 flat, base the "frame" around the clock front and back with Red Violet (1). With a ¼-inch (19mm) wash brush, give the top, sides and bottom of the clock two coats of Red Violet mixed with a little flow medium. Using a no. 6 flat and Red Violet, paint the clock hole and an ⅛-inch (3mm) band around the face (2). Give these areas two coats. Allow to dry. With a 10/0 round and Antique Green plus a little flow medium, paint little dashes over the edge of the Red Violet bands around the face and on the front and back of the clock (3). Copy the design onto tracing paper and transfer using the chalk method (page 15). Using a 10/0 liner, paint the Red Violet details on the leaves as shown (4), then use a 10/0 round to fill the leaves with Rich Gold (5). Use Red Violet and a no. 2 filbert to paint the

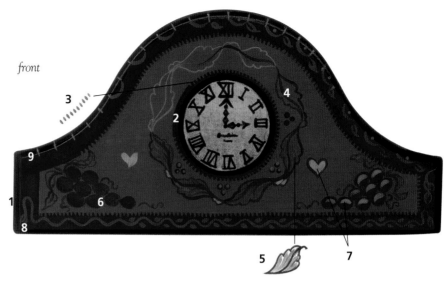

front

grapes and a 10/0 round to paint the other details (6). Add highlights to the grapes and fill in the hearts with Vellum on a mini filbert. Outline the hearts with Red Violet on a 10/0 round (7). Paint the

Antique Green details with a 10/0 liner (8). Use chalk to mark off the strokes along the top, then paint as shown using Antique Green and a 10/0 round (9). The gold dots are added in step two.

top

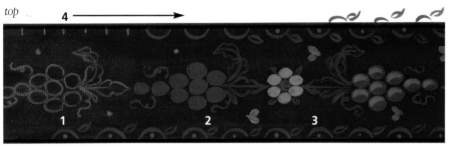

progression of grape leaves

sides

2 The Top and Sides of the Clock

To paint the top and sides of the clock, copy the design onto tracing paper and transfer using the chalk method (1). Use Antique Green and a no. 2 filbert to paint the grapes and a 10/0 round to paint the leaves and tendrils (2). Paint the flower and hearts and highlight the grapes with the mini filbert and Vellum. Use a 10/0 round and Rich Gold to fill in the grape leaves and flower center (3). Connect the top vine to the front and back vine, painting as shown with a 10/0 round and thinned Antique Green. Add the Rich Gold dots with a small stylus (4).

3 The Clock Back

Transfer the design to the back. Paint as shown using a 10/0 liner. Allow to dry. Wipe the clock with a damp cloth, then spray the entire surface with Krylon Matte Finish Spray, no. 1311.

4 Adding the Screen Pattern

Lay the clock over the piece of screen (make sure the lines of the screen are straight) and cut a separate piece for each side, making the piece a little larger than the sides. Hold a piece of screen over one side, make sure the lines are straight, then drybrush over the screen using a ¾-inch (19mm) wash brush and Provincial Beige. Hold the brush straight up and lightly brush back and forth over the top. It's best to practice first. Do not move the screen. Work in small areas, using a light touch. If you make a mistake you can easily wipe it off and start over. Allow to dry, then spray with Krylon Crystal Clear Acrylic Spray.

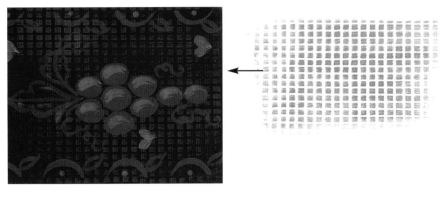

5 The Switch Plate

When the back of the switch plate is dry, paint the frame around the plate with two coats of Red Violet and a little flow medium on a no. 8 flat (1). Transfer the basic design using the chalk method, then dust with a mop brush (2). Stroke over all of basic elements, except in the frame area, with single strokes of Red Violet, using a 10/0 liner, mini filbert and a 10/0 round as indicated at right (3). Continue to build the Red Violet strokes as shown (4). Next add the Rich Gold overstrokes using a 10/0 round, then the Vellum areas as shown (5). Follow the progression shown at right to paint the Antique Green strokework along the top and bottom of the frame using a mini filbert and a 10/0 liner (6). Complete the top and bottom of the frame as shown along the bottom section (7). Start the grapes by outlining the vines with a 10/0 liner and thinned Antique Green. Add the grapes as shown using a mini filbert (8). Follow the sequence shown at right rather than doing them all at once. Use a 10/0 round to finish the strokework with Rich Gold (9). After the switch plate is dry, wipe with a damp cloth and spray with Krylon Matte Finish Spray, no. 1311. Cut a piece of screen larger than the switch plate, place it over the plate with the lines straight and secure with 3M Long-Mask Masking Tape. Drybrush as described for the clock. When this is dry, dust off and spray with Krylon Crystal

Clear Acrylic Spray. Finally, add the tacks or screws. I used old-fashioned tacks that I painted to match the surface. Poke the tacks into a small piece of Styrofoam. Brush them with sealer or primer, dry, then base with Red Violet. When dry, drybrush with Rich Gold, dry again and spray with Krylon Crystal Clear.

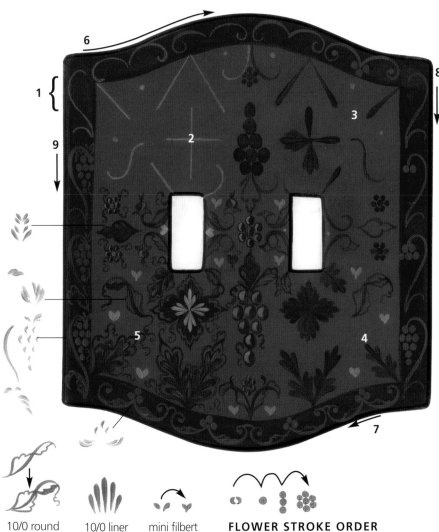

10/0 round   10/0 liner   mini filbert   **FLOWER STROKE ORDER**
mini filbert

Hallingdal Sewing Box

My two remarkable grandmothers, Marie and Gramzy, taught me a love for sewing. Marie was a seamstress. Ladies would come to her with their fashion problems and she would fix them. It was amazing to watch her. I remember one year I wanted a dress like Cinderella for Christmas. I drew her a picture and, sure enough, before Christmas my dream dress arrived. I've enjoyed doing the same kind of thing for my daughters.

Gramzy was the "mender." She had to get by on very little, but you'd never guess it. No matter how big the hole in your socks, she'd fix it and the mend job would hold up better than the sock!

This little box is filled with a few memories of the tools they used. I chose one of my favorite traditional painting styles for this set. It's a form of Rosemaling (Norwegian folk painting) called Hallingdal.

Preparing the Surfaces

1 Follow the basic wood preparation instructions on page 14. Base the entire oval box with two coats of Spice and the entire lid with two coats of Gold Oxide. Use a little flow medium and a ¾-inch (19mm) wash brush. Sand with a 3M Sanding Sponge between coats.
2 Base the thimble and needle box with Carbon Black and a little flow medium on a no. 6 flat. Hold the needle box with a Q-tip while you paint it. You can also paint the inside with the Q-tip.
3 Base the large and small spools with two coats of Storm Blue and a little flow medium on a no. 10 flat. Again use the Q-tip to paint the spool hole.

MATERIALS

SURFACES
- 4" × 5¼" × 3" (10.2cm × 13.3cm × 7.6cm) oval bentwood box
- small pill box
- 2¼" × ½" (5.7cm × 1.3cm) needle box
- 2⅛" ×1½" (5.4cm × 3.8cm) and 1⅛" × 1½" (2.9cm × 3.8cm) spools
- 1⅛" × 1" (2.9cm × 2.5cm) thimble

ADDITIONS TO BASIC SUPPLIES
- small stencil sponge
- soft cloth

- 8½" × 11" (21.6cm × 27.9cm) sheet of cardstock or Bristol board

BRUSHES
- ¾-inch (19mm) wash brush
- no. 4, no. 6, no. 10 and no. 12 flats
- no. 2 and no. 4 filberts
- ¼-inch (6mm) and ⅛-inch (3mm) angles
- 10/0 Dressden liner
- 10/0, 2/0, no. 0 and no. 2 rounds
- 2/0 scroller liner

COLOR PALETTE

Jo Sonja's Smoked Pearl

Jo Sonja's Yellow Oxide

Jo Sonja's Gold Oxide

Jo Sonja's Background Color Spice

Jo Sonja's Napthol Crimson

Jo Sonja's Indian Red Oxide

Jo Sonja's Celadon

Jo Sonja's Olive Green

Jo Sonja's Raw Umber

Jo Sonja's Storm Blue

Jo Sonja's Carbon Black

Jo Sonja's Burnt Sienna

4 Base the little button box with two coats of Burnt Sienna mixed with flow medium on a no. 10 flat. The Dry-It Board comes in handy here.

Applying the Scallops
We're going to make a scalloped-edge template. This is an easy and accurate way to put the scallops on.
1 Copy the scallop pattern onto tracing paper.

2 Place carbon paper carbon side down onto cardstock and place the scallop design over it. With a stylus or pencil, copy the scallops onto the cardstock.
3 Cut the scalloped edge out.
4 With a chalk pencil, draw scallops, points down, along the bottom edge of the oval box. You might want to plan out where the scallops land before you begin to make sure they'll be even.

These patterns and designs may be hand-traced or photocopied for personal use only. Shown at full size.

DESIGN FOR TOP OF LID

DESIGN FOR SIDE OF OVAL BOX

BUTTON BOX LID

DESIGN FOR INSIDE OF LID

SCALLOP PATTERN

Krilling

One of the first faux techniques I learned was in a Rosemaling class. The teacher referred to the use of marking over the antique mixture as "Krilling." We're going to krill along the sides and on the underside of the oval lid, around the inside of the box, along the scallops, on the bottom of the box and along the sides of the small button box.

1 All areas to be krilled must be glazed first to help the krilling go on more smoothly. Use Jo Sonja's Clear Glazing Medium and flat brushes to fit each area. Dry thoroughly.

2 Mix 6 parts Raw Umber plus 1 part Burnt Sienna. Create an antiquing mixture by mixing the above colors with an equal amount of retarder using a bent palette knife.

3 Brush the antiquing mixture over the areas to be krilled using a ¾-inch (19mm) wash brush.

4 Dab a little antiquing mixture onto a small, *dry* stencil sponge—don't swish or overload the sponge. Practice gently twisting the sponge over a piece of cardstock, holding the sponge handle upright. Now move to the antiqued area and twist to create a pattern in the wet glaze, working quickly in 3-inch (7.6cm) sections. Allow to dry overnight.

Before you begin painting the design, you might want to practice and see which brushes go with which strokes. Refer to the Stroke Worksheet on this page and page 90 as needed. Strokework is easier when pulled down or toward you. Turn your object as you go. I've added dots with a stylus where needed.

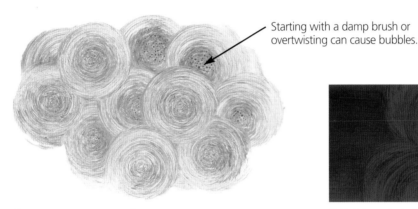

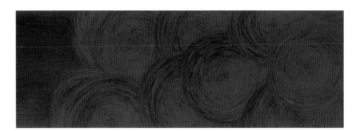
Starting with a damp brush or overtwisting can cause bubbles.

Twist the sponge to create a swirl pattern.

This is how the krilling will look over the base color.

Stroke Worksheet

10/0 Dressden liner

10/0 round

Stroke Worksheet Continued

Aim for one long stroke. If this is too hard, break into two.

start with middle

2/0 scroller

2/0 round

no. 0 round

no. 2 filbert

¼-inch (6mm) angle

no. 4 filbert

no. 2 round

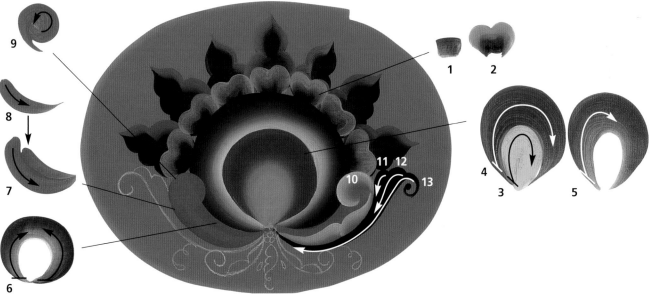

1 The Oval Box Lid

Copy the design to tracing paper and use the chalk method (page 15) to transfer it to the top of the lid. Dust off (1). Use a ¼-inch (6mm) angle and Olive Green to paint the bottom half of the leaves as shown (2). Reload with Olive Green and paint the upper half of the leaves (3). The middle three leaves are shaped slightly differently. After basing all leaves, go back to the first leaf and repeat with a second coat with flow medium added. Keep the paint smooth and the strokes the same (4). Highlight both edges of the center leaf with a ¼-inch (6mm) angle double loaded with Smoked Pearl and Olive Green, keeping the green toward the center of the leaf (5). Repeat to highlight only the inside edge of the leaf on either side of the center leaf (6). Shade the outer edge of these two leaves with a double load of Raw Umber and Olive Green, again keeping the green toward the center of the leaf (7). Use the same technique to highlight the outer leaves using Celadon and Olive Green (8). Shade the outer leaves with Storm Blue and Olive Green. Always keep the green toward the center of the leaf (9).

❧ Hint ❧

• I almost always moisten my brush with flow medium before loading with color.

• I find it best to blend double loads on my disposable palette. You'll go through more palette paper this way, but the waxy film helps the paint stay in the brush so you'll use less paint.

2

Use a ¼-inch (6mm) angle to put a little Raw Umber base where the petals go. Rinse, then double load the brush with Yellow Oxide and Raw Umber. Go over the Raw Umber, trying not to overlap the petals (1). Dry, then repeat the double load. Mix Yellow Oxide with a drop of retarder using a palette knife and load on a no. 10 flat, keeping the bristles together to form a sharp edge (2). Keeping the handle straight up, place the brush at the angle shown and follow the small arrow up, stop, pivot and come back down, then angle off (3). Rinse the brush and blot off, then load with a mix of Indian Red Oxide and a drop of retarder. Pull a larger loop along the outside of the Yellow Oxide loop (4). Moisten a no. 10 flat with retarder, double load with Yellow Oxide and Indian Red Oxide and blend over the previous step (5). Moisten a no. 10 flat with a little retarder and go around the center. Mix a drop of retarder into a puddle of Storm Blue and into a puddle of Smoked Pearl. Dampen a no. 10 flat and double load with these colors. Place the brush at the lines as shown and follow around to the top (6). If you have trouble completing one side in a single stroke, you can do it in two strokes—go halfway up, reload, then do the other half and blend together. If you can see the background too much or want a better blend, let it dry and go over it again. Moisten a no. 4 filbert with flow medium and load the brush with Celadon. Make the understrokes as shown (7). Repeat with a smaller second stroke on top (8). Reload and paint the "knob" on top (9). Highlight these strokes using a retarder-moistened no. 4 filbert double loaded with Smoked Pearl and Celadon (10). Mix Carbon Black with Indian Red Oxide to make a richer black. Paint the top small stroke (11), then the second stroke (12) using a no. 2 filbert. Load a 2/0 scroller (liner) with the black mix (thin with flow medium as needed) and paint the final stroke (13).

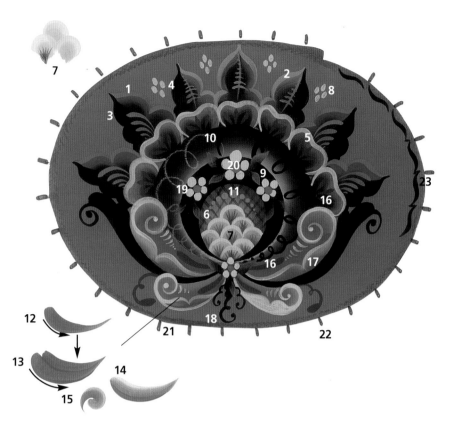

3 Refer to the stroke worksheet for help in making these strokes. Thin all mixes with flow medium. Retarder also works well for linework, but it does increase the drying time. Paint the outer leaf highlights as shown with a 10/0 liner and Celadon plus Smoked Pearl (1). Use a 10/0 liner and Olive Green plus Smoked Pearl to paint the center leaf highlights (2). Use a 10/0 liner to shadow the outer leaves using a mix of Carbon Black plus Indian Red Oxide (3). Mix Raw Umber plus Carbon Black to shade the upper side leaves using a 10/0 liner (4). Highlight the petals using a 10/0 liner and Yellow Oxide plus Smoked Pearl (5). Use Raw Umber and a 2/0 scroller (liner) to crosshatch the center area (6). Double load a moistened no. 4 flat with Smoked Pearl and Yellow Oxide. Start with the center back petal and work forward. Add little shadows with Raw Umber on a 10/0 round. Highlight the tops of the petals

with Yellow Oxide plus Smoked Pearl and a 10/0 round (7). Use the same mix and brush to make the dot diamonds above the leaves (8). Use a no. 2 round and Carbon Black plus Indian Red Oxide to paint the center "igloo" (9). If you can't do it all in one stroke, go halfway up on each side and connect at the top. When the rest of the painting is dry, transfer the spiral using the chalk method and a stylus. Dust off, then paint the spiral with a 2/0 scroller and Carbon Black plus Indian Red Oxide (10). Using a large stylus or the end of a small paintbrush and thinned Yellow Oxide, tap the center dot, then go down each side without reloading (11). Add the bottom scrolls as shown, using a no. 2 filbert and Celadon (12-13). Then highlight with a double load of Smoked Pearl and Celadon (14-15). Add Indian Red Oxide strokes to the petals using a 10/0 round. Add Indian Red Oxide scrolls with a 10/0 liner

(16). Highlight the Celadon scrolls with Smoked Pearl linework using a 10/0 liner (17). Add black curlicues with a 10/0 round and Indian Red Oxide curlicues with a 10/0 liner. Double load an ⅛-inch (3mm) angle with Yellow Oxide on top and Olive Green on bottom. Paint all leaves as shown (18). Add dot flower petals with Smoked Pearl and an EZ Dotz tool, brush handle tip or 2/0 scroller brush (the latter creates a more handpainted look) (19). Allow the petals to dry, then dot on the centers with Napthol Crimson (20). Go around the edge of the lid with a little antique mix (page 89). Allow to dry (21). Using a piece of chalk, mark off the edge as shown (22). Using a 2/0 scroller or 10/0 liner and Carbon Black plus Indian Red Oxide, make **S**-strokes between the marks, then connect with a line (23). Set aside to dry overnight.

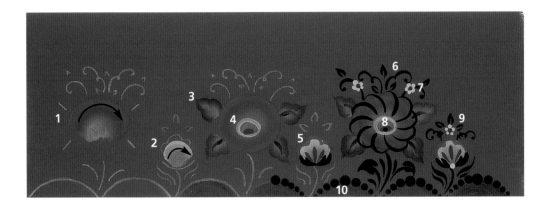

4 Finishing the Side of the Box

Copy one large and one small flower motif to tracing paper. Cut apart. Use the chalk method to trace the flowers between the scallops. Dust off. Moisten a no. 6 flat with retarder, blot, then double load with half Celadon and half Yellow Oxide mixed with Smoked Pearl. Paint the morning glories all in one stroke or half at a time (1). Moisten a no. 4 flat with retarder, blot off, then double load with Smoked Pearl on top and Yellow Oxide mixed with Smoked Pearl on the bottom. Paint one-third of a circle for each bud (2). Add leaves using an ⅛-inch (3mm) angle double loaded with Olive Green and Yellow Oxide (3). Add a little ring inside the flowers with a 10/0 round and Yellow Oxide plus Smoked Pearl. Paint the center with Indian Red Oxide (4). Use a 10/0 round and Indian Red Oxide to paint three strokes in the middle of each bud. Paint Carbon Black plus

Indian Red Oxide strokes on the bottom of the bud, then line the upper edge with Celadon (5). Use a 10/0 round and Carbon Black plus Indian Red Oxide to add the details (6). With a small stylus and Smoked Pearl, paint dot petals. Dry, then add Indian Red Oxide centers (7). Add small black dots to the flower centers with a stylus (8). Finish the detail for the bud with a 10/0 round and Carbon Black plus Indian Red Oxide. Add dot flowers as you did for the large flowers (9). Finish the scalloped bottom with Raw Umber dots as shown (10).

5 The Inside of the Lid

Use the chalk method and a stylus to transfer the design. With a 10/0 liner and Raw Umber, paint the outline. Make sure you have the lid the right way so you don't paint it upside down!

6 The Accessories

I only included one pattern for the small accessories. The rest are painted without patterns, using the lessons taught in this project. Trace the pattern to the top of the button box using the chalk method. Use Smoked Pearl, Yellow Oxide, Olive Green and the black mix to paint the box. Use a no. 2 filbert (to fill in the petals), a 10/0 round and 10/0 liner.

7 Finishing

After everything has dried for twenty-four hours, use J.W. etc. Right-Step Satin Varnish to finish the oval box and Krylon Crystal Clear Acrylic Spray for the small pieces. Wax the box after another twenty-four hours if desired. Line the bottom inside of the boxes with black flock.

Matryoshka Dolls

*M*atryoshka—even the name sounds intriguing! A Matryoshka is the name used for wooden nesting dolls made in Russia. The name itself means "mother" or "motherhood." These dolls first originated in China around the 1800s. They were presented to St. Petersburg in 1896 in an exhibition of Japanese art. The dolls were mainly used for toys and usually told a story.

Nesting dolls are now made worldwide. The Russian versions are the most popular due to the fantastic artwork created by Russian artists.

This is another subject I truly love working with. You can have so much fun creating your own story—or even painting your own family. (Unfortunately, I haven't found a set large enough to depict my family!)

On this set I painted "The Story of George" for my oldest daughter, Trudi. George was a stray cat that adopted our family. Because of health problems, we couldn't have a pet indoors. Trudi worried about George being alone outside every night. All summer he got the royal treatment, and earned his keep by getting rid of all the mice. By Christmas, George had taken up residence in Trudi's room with the stipulation that he would return outside as soon as the snow melted. Of course, that didn't happen! George remained with our family for several more seasons. He was laid to rest as a much-loved family pet.

Preparing the Dolls

1 Every set of dolls is slightly different and not one is totally perfect (this gives them character). Put the dolls together to see how they fit. If the halves are tight, sand the lip with fine sandpaper. Next, check how they sit. If they wobble, sand the bases flat. Fill any holes with wood filler.

2 Follow the instructions for wood prep on page 14. When you apply

MATERIALS

SURFACES
- nesting doll set—my dolls are 1¾-inch (4.5cm), 2½-inch (6.4cm), 3¼-inch (8.3cm), 4-inch (10.2cm) and 5½-inch (14cm)

ADDITIONS TO BASIC SUPPLIES
- single-edge razor blade

BRUSHES
- old no. 2 filbert
- ¾-inch (19mm) wash brush
- no. 2, no. 4, no. 6, no. 8, no. 10 and no. 12 flats
- mini and no. 2 filberts
- 20/0 and 2/0 Dressden liners
- 10/0, 20/0 and no. 0 rounds

COLOR PALETTE

Ceramcoat
Quaker Grey (QG)

Jo Sonja's
Background Color
Blossom (Bl)

Jo Sonja's
Background Color
Primrose (P)

Jo Sonja's
Background Color
Azure (A)

Jo Sonja's
Background Color
Lavender (L)

Ceramcoat
White (W)

Ceramcoat
Ice Storm Violet
(ISV)

Americana
Taffy Cream (TC)

Ceramcoat
Rose Petal Pink
(RPP)

Americana
Grey Sky (GS)

Americana
French Mauve (FM)

Jo Sonja's
Turners Yellow (TY)

Jo Sonja's
Skin Tone Base
(STB)

Ceramcoat
Sunbright Yellow
(SY)

Ceramcoat
Wild Rose (WR)

Ceramcoat
Cactus Green (CG)

Ceramcoat
Caribbean Blue
(CB)

FolkArt
Medium Orange
(MO)

FolkArt
Clover (C)

Americana
Baby Blue (BB)

Ceramcoat
Pretty Pink (PP)

FolkArt
Fresh Foliage (FF)

Americana
Cadmium Red (CR)

Americana
Honey Brown
(HB)

Americana
Antique Mauve
(AM)

Ceramcoat
Territorial
Beige (TB)

Americana
Kelly Green (KG)

FolkArt
Medium Gray
(MG)

FolkArt
Indigo
(I)

Americana
Wedgewood Blue
(WB)

FolkArt
Night Sky (NS)

Americana Hauser
Dark Green (HDG)

Ceramcoat Brown
Velvet
(BV)

Ceramcoat
Dark Burnt Umber
(DBU)

Ceramcoat
Black (B)

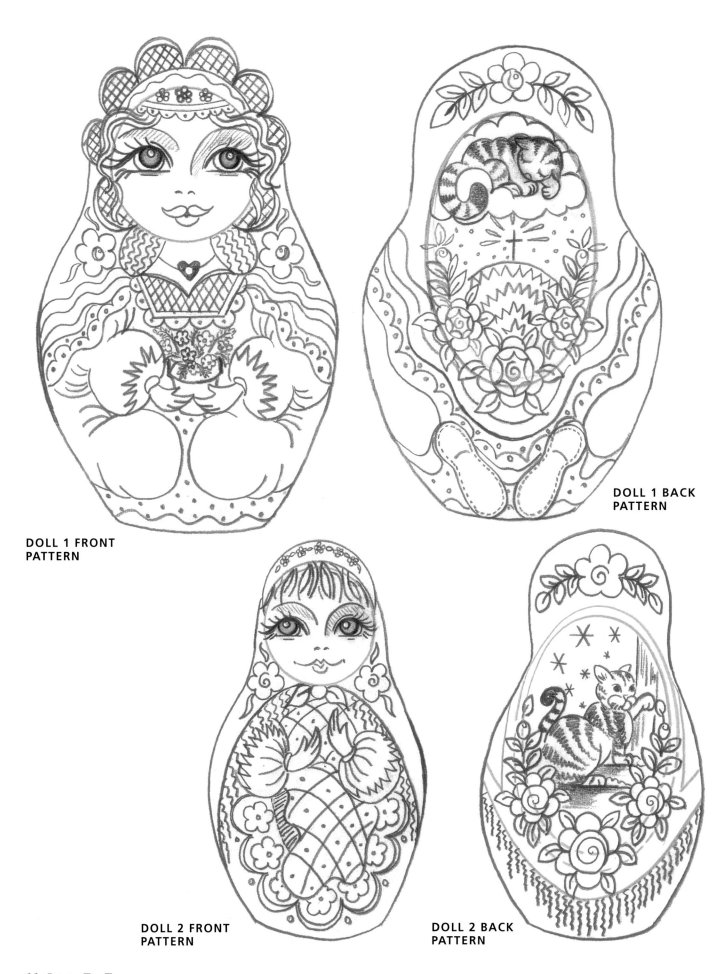

DOLL 1 FRONT PATTERN

DOLL 1 BACK PATTERN

DOLL 2 FRONT PATTERN

DOLL 2 BACK PATTERN

DOLL 3 FRONT PATTERN

DOLL 3 BACK PATTERN

DOLL 4 FRONT PATTERN

DOLL 4 BACK PATTERN

DOLL 5 FRONT PATTERN

DOLL 5 BACK PATTERN

The patterns and designs on pages 96-97 may be hand-traced or photocopied for personal use only. Shown at full size.

sealer, and through every painting step, keep the two halves of each doll together; don't take them apart. When you're finished, you'll cut them open. You won't be painting the inside or the lip.

General Painting Instructions

It would take another book to give instructions for painting every detail on these dolls. Instead, I'll just give general painting instructions. To find out what colors to use, match each element on the dolls to the color swatches alongside each step. The color abbreviations are listed on page 95. This project is intended for someone who has a little more experience.

1 Basecoat each doll with the color indicated on the following pages. Use two thin coats, sanding in between with an extra-fine 3M Sanding Sponge to smooth. Apply a third coat. Normally I draw the basic design on first and base individual colors separately. This keeps the surface from getting too bumpy; however, it's more difficult to paint this way, so we're starting with a solid basecoat. Any unwanted ridges can be sanded smooth with a 3M Sanding Sponge, then given another coat of paint mixed with flow medium. After you've based each doll, allow to dry two hours.

2 Next base the faces and necks with two coats of Skin Tone Base plus flow medium. Refer to the individual doll instructions for the proper brush. Sand with a 3M Sanding Sponge lightly, then apply a third coat.

3 Paint the oval on the back of each "babushka" (kerchief or scarf) using the color and brush directed in the individual doll instructions. This area is sometimes used to tell a story, as in this case. Then use a chalk pencil to draw the smaller oval on, making sure it's directly behind the head and not off center. Give this oval two to three

coats of the color specified using the appropriate flat brush.

4 It's almost impossible to trace the entire pattern over the dolls. It's better to trace the face and the oval and draw the rest on using a chalk pencil. Copy the face and the oval scene to tracing paper and cut out. Use the CPC method (page 15) for the face and the chalk method for the ovals. Dust off.

5 Next we'll shade the facial features using chalk pastels (see page 15). Rub a brown pastel on sandpaper, then brush the dust under the eyebrows as shown below with an old no. 2 filbert. Dust the brown out of the brush with your fingers—don't rinse the brush. After you paint the eyes on, go back

and add rosy cheeks with dark pink pastel dust.

6 Now you're ready to start the details. It's best to start with the largest doll and work your way down. The smaller the doll gets, the less detail she has.

7 When all the dolls have dried at least overnight, remove the chalk lines and spray with Krylon Crystal Clear Acrylic Spray. After the dolls have had a chance to cure at least twenty-four hours, follow around the line that separates the two halves of each doll with the razor blade. If the halves won't come apart right away, give them a gentle twist. If that doesn't work, try the razor again. Keep the cut clean—you don't want ragged edges. Wax if desired.

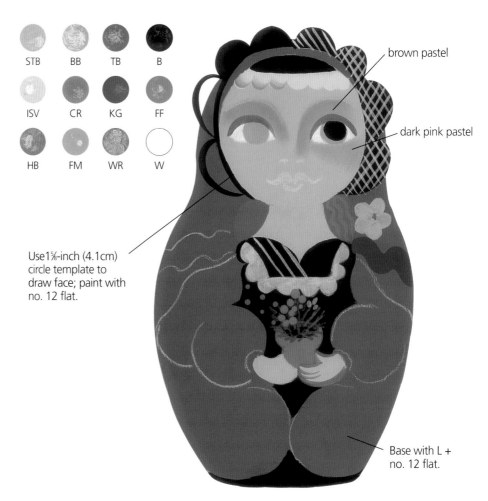

brown pastel

dark pink pastel

Use 1⅝-inch (4.1cm) circle template to draw face; paint with no. 12 flat.

Base with L + no. 12 flat.

DOLL 1 BASING FRONT

STB BB TB B

ISV CR KG FF

HB FM WR W

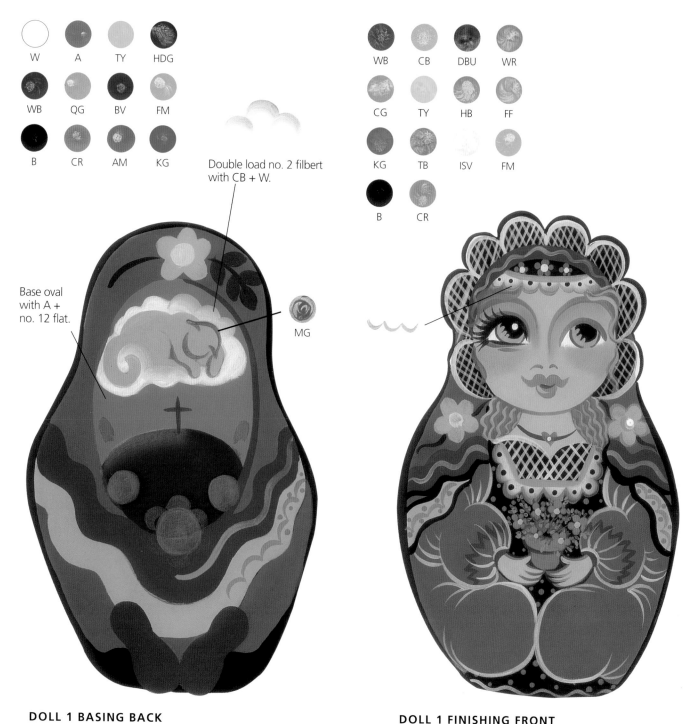

W   A   TY   HDG

WB   QG   BV   FM

B   CR   AM   KG

WB   CB   DBU   WR

CG   TY   HB   FF

KG   TB   ISV   FM

B   CR

Double load no. 2 filbert with CB + W.

Base oval with A + no. 12 flat.

MG

DOLL 1 BASING BACK

DOLL 1 FINISHING FRONT

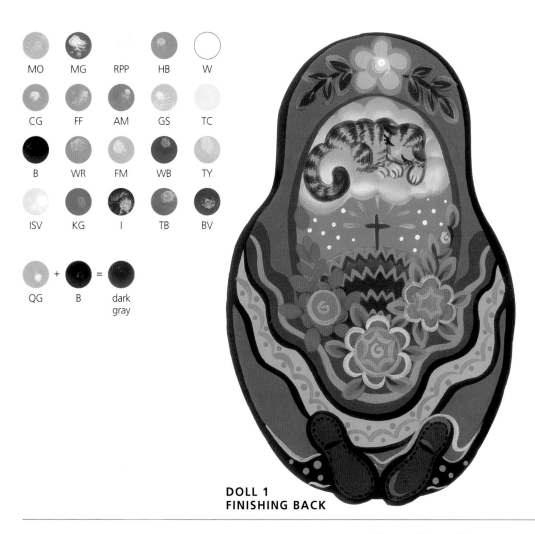

MO MG RPP HB W
CG FF AM GS TC
B WR FM WB TY
ISV KG I TB BV

QG + B = dark gray

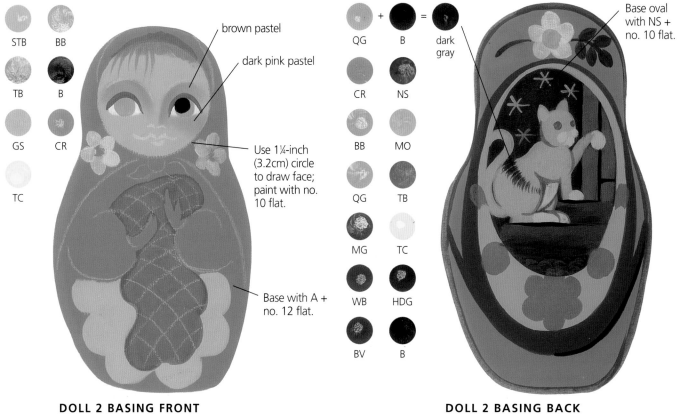

**DOLL 1
FINISHING BACK**

STB BB
TB B
GS CR
TC

brown pastel

dark pink pastel

Use 1¼-inch (3.2cm) circle to draw face; paint with no. 10 flat.

Base with A + no. 12 flat.

DOLL 2 BASING FRONT

QG + B = dark gray
CR NS
BB MO
QG TB
MG TC
WB HDG
BV B

Base oval with NS + no. 10 flat.

DOLL 2 BASING BACK

DOLL 2 FINISHING FRONT

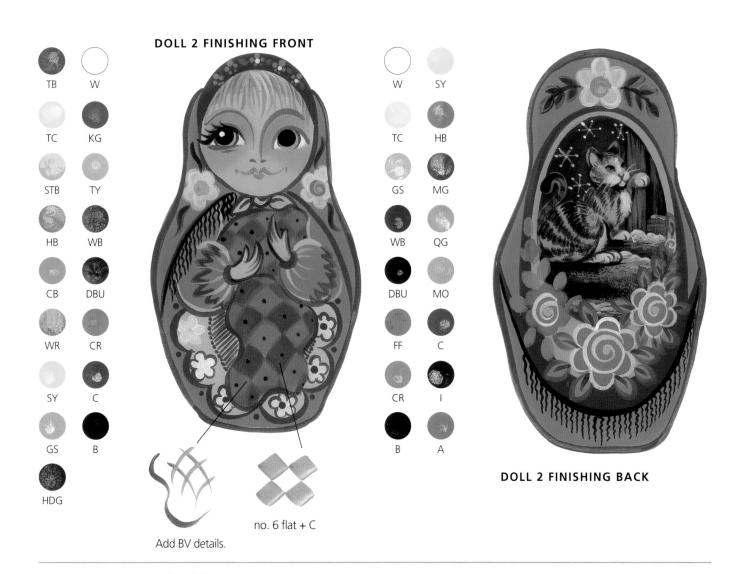

TB · W
TC · KG
STB · TY
HB · WB
CB · DBU
WR · CR
SY · C
GS · B
HDG

W · SY
TC · HB
GS · MG
WB · QG
DBU · MO
FF · C
CR · I
B · A

no. 6 flat + C

Add BV details.

DOLL 2 FINISHING BACK

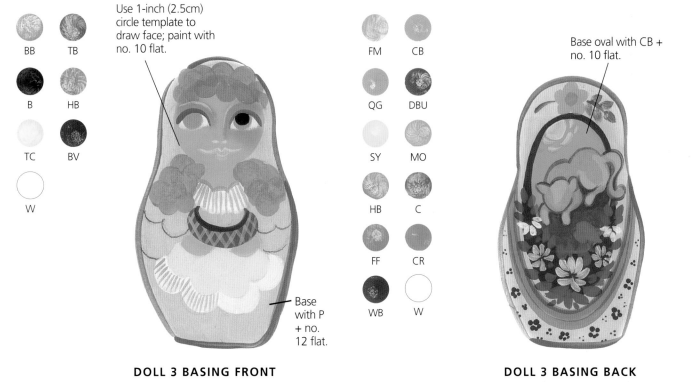

BB · TB
B · HB
TC · BV
W

FM · CB
QG · DBU
SY · MO
HB · C
FF · CR
WB · W

Use 1-inch (2.5cm) circle template to draw face; paint with no. 10 flat.

Base with P + no. 12 flat.

Base oval with CB + no. 10 flat.

DOLL 3 BASING FRONT

DOLL 3 BASING BACK

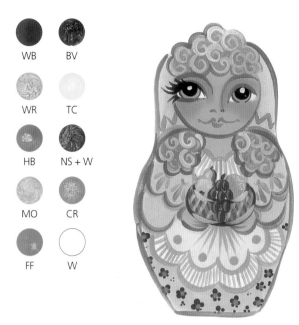

WB   BV

WR   TC

HB   NS + W

MO   CR

FF   W

DOLL 3 FINISHING FRONT

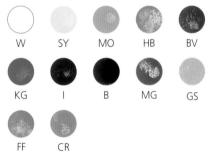

W   SY   MO   HB   BV

KG   I   B   MG   GS

FF   CR

**DOLL 3 FINISHING
BACK**

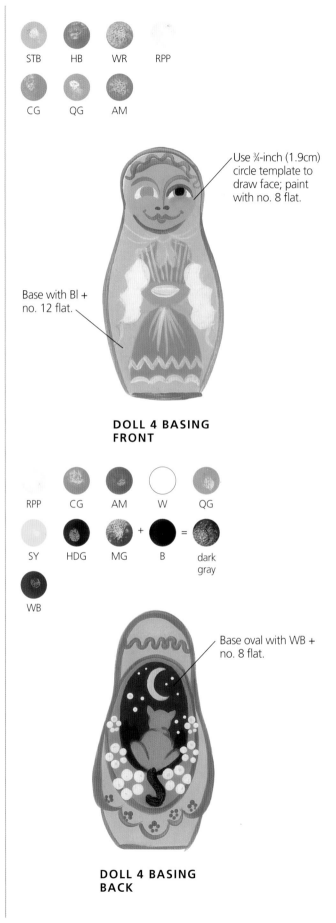

STB   HB   WR   RPP

CG   QG   AM

Use ¾-inch (1.9cm)
circle template to
draw face; paint
with no. 8 flat.

Base with Bl +
no. 12 flat.

**DOLL 4 BASING
FRONT**

RPP   CG   AM   W   QG

SY   HDG   MG + B = dark gray

WB

Base oval with WB +
no. 8 flat.

**DOLL 4 BASING
BACK**

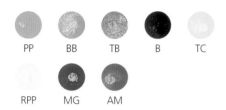

PP BB TB B TC

RPP MG AM

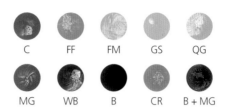

C FF FM GS QG

MG WB B CR B + MG

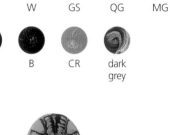

WB W GS QG MG

I B CR dark grey

DOLL 4 FINISHING FRONT

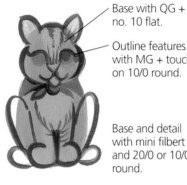

Base with QG + no. 10 flat.

Outline features with MG + touch B on 10/0 round.

Base and detail with mini filbert and 20/0 or 10/0 round.

DOLL 5 BASING FRONT

DOLL 5 BASING BACK

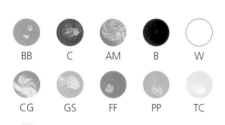

BB C AM B W

CG GS FF PP TC

RPP

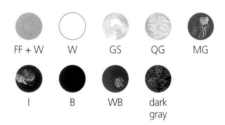

FF + W W GS QG MG

I B WB dark gray

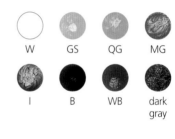

W GS QG MG

I B WB dark gray

DOLL 5 FINISHING FRONT

DOLL 5 FINISHING BACK

DOLL 4 FINISHING BACK

Mini Russian Tray

*T*his little tray is a spin-off of Zhostovo floral painting. Zhostovo is a village near Moscow where this style of painting developed, with roots stemming from lacquered miniatures.

With the takeover of the Soviet regime, the small, mostly family-owned workshops producing these trays were joined together to form a factory near Zhostovo. Instead of having one artist paint one tray, different levels of painters began to specialize in certain areas. First the tray is manufactured and cured, then basecoated several times. After a careful sanding, it's given to a painter who basecoats the design. Next, a master artist completes the composition, then another artist adds the borders. The final step is the lacquer finish.

The tray we're going to do doesn't compare to the Russian originals, but it is a stepping-stone to understanding and appreciating the elegance the Zhostovo style offers.

Preparing a Metal Surface
The surface you use will determine your first steps. You should try to find a small metal piece, but even a wooden box will do.
1 For metal, first buff it with fine steel wool.
2 Wash the piece in hot, soapy water, rinse well and dry off.
3 After it's dry, spray with black metal primer.
4 When dry, give it two to three coats of flat black spray paint.

Preparing a Wood Surface
1 If you're using wood, such as the small duck decoy shown on page 104, follow the wood prep instructions (page 14).
2 Give the piece two to three coats of Black acrylic mixed with a little flow medium. Use the wash brush. Lightly sand between coats with an extra-fine 3M Sanding Sponge.

MATERIALS

SURFACES
- small tin or wooden tray or other small surface

ADDITIONS TO BASIC SUPPLIES
- medium-stiff plastic, like a large candy wrapper
- soft cloth
- fine steel wool
- Krylon Ultra Flat Black Spray, no. 1602
- Krylon All-Purpose Black Spray Primer, no. 1316

BRUSHES
- ¾-inch (19mm) wash brush
- no.10 flat
- mini and no. 2 filberts
- 10/0 Dressden liner
- 10/0 round

COLOR PALETTE

Jo Sonja's
Unbleached
Titanium

Jo Sonja's
Naples Yellow Hue

Jo Sonja's
Yellow Oxide

Jo Sonja's
Provincial Beige

Jo Sonja's
Norwegian Orange

Jo Sonja's
Moss Green

Jo Sonja's
Green Oxide

Jo Sonja's
Pine Green

Jo Sonja's
Brilliant Violet

Jo Sonja's
Trans Magenta

Jo Sonja's
Red Violet

Jo Sonja's
Permanent
Alizarine

Jo Sonja's
Dioxazine Purple

Jo Sonja's
Purple Madder

Jo Sonja's
Silver

Jo Sonja's
Rich Gold

Americana
Mississippi Mud

Americana
Charcoal Grey

FolkArt Metallics
Sequin Black

Ceramcoat
Black

This design may be hand-traced or photocopied for personal use only. Shown at full size. Use half the design if painting a smaller item, like the duck decoy.

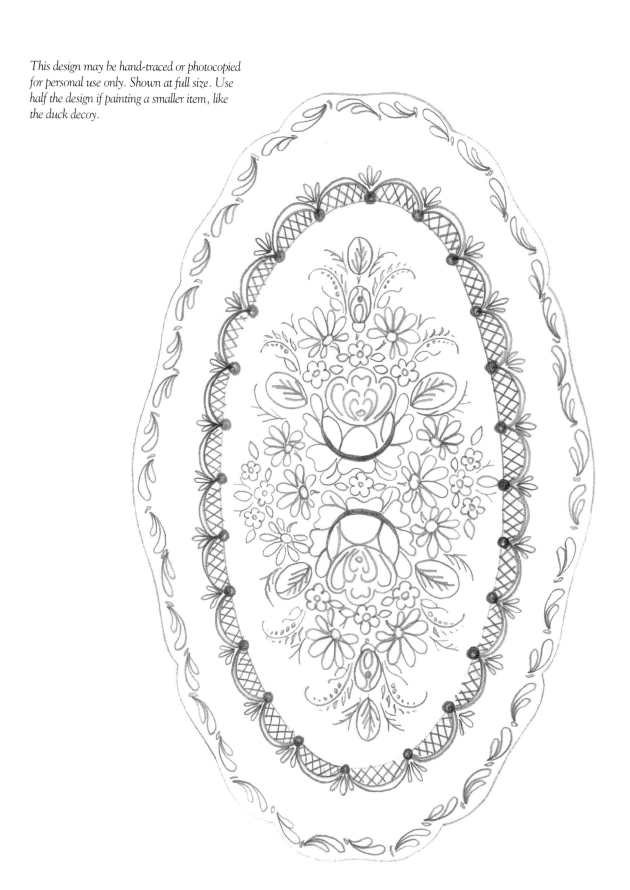

1 Basing the Tray and Painting the Border

With a ¾-inch (19mm) wash brush and a no. 10 flat, give the edge and back of the tray one coat of Sequin Black (1). Add a little flow medium to Mississippi Mud and apply two coats to the center oval of the tray with the wash brush (2). Allow to dry. With a palette knife, mix six parts Jo Sonja's Matte Finishing Varnish to one part Charcoal Grey. Rub retarder over the center oval. Crumple or twist a piece of plastic. A large candy wrapper is ideal; it should be stiffer than plastic wrap but not as stiff as a chip bag. Dip the plastic in the grey mix, test to be sure the color is right, then pounce gently over the retarder (3). Pouncing too hard or a runny mix will create bubbles. Remove the texturing immediately and start over if you're not happy with it. Dry completely. You may want to spray the tray with Krylon Matte Finish Spray, no. 1311 at this point so the background won't be damaged if you need to wipe off a mistake later. Using a chalk pencil to mark the divisions, divide the edge of the oval into fourths. Divide each fourth in half, then divide each of these halves into three equal sections (4). Using Mississippi Mud and a 10/0 liner, paint scallops between the marks you just made (5). Add crosshatch lines inside the scallops (6), then add three strokes (7) and a stylus dot between each scallop (8). Now divide the outer rim as shown. Use a mix of two parts Rich Gold and one part Silver and a 10/0 liner to paint these strokes (9).

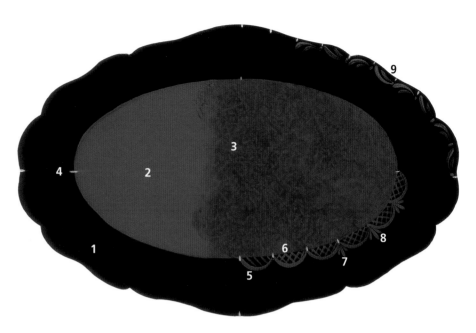

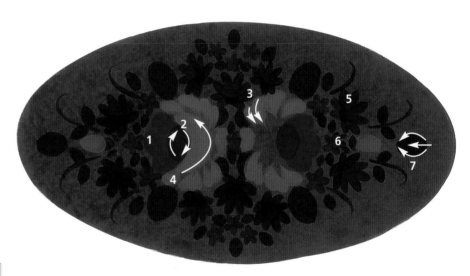

⚜ Hint ⚜

In Zhostovo painting, a tint (white plus a little color) or white is normally used to base each element. If you want a brighter, lighter tray, base the flowers with white or a light color and overstroke with more color. Also note that the color in the center tends to be brighter than the outer edge.

---

2 Basing the Floral Design

Use the chalk method (page 15) to transfer the design to the oval. Dust off with a mop brush. Using a no. 2 filbert and Permanent Alizarine, form the back petals of the roses; start with the middle stroke, then add the side strokes (1). With a no. 2 filbert and Purple Madder, form the center of the rose with two strokes (2). Use a no. 2 filbert and Provincial Beige to stroke the rest of the rose petals (3), then to add the bowl of the rose (4) and the buds. Go over these strokes in the same manner to strengthen the base. With a mini filbert and Purple Madder, base the echinacea (5). Using Dioxazine Purple and a mini filbert, base the violets (6). Base the leaves and lily stems with a mini filbert and Pine Green (7). If you want to strengthen the colors, go over them again.

3 Put some blending medium on your palette. Use as needed for transparency as you overstroke. Brush mix a little Yellow Oxide into Naples Yellow Hue and go over the roses and buds with a no. 2 filbert (1). Mix Red Violet and Unbleached Titanium and overstroke the echinacea with a mini filbert (2). Overstroke the violets with Brilliant Violet and a mini filbert (3). Apply Permanent Alizarine to the leaves as shown, using a mini filbert (4). Add Purple Madder centers to the buds with a mini filbert (5).

I made these centers with a stylus; they look unnatural.

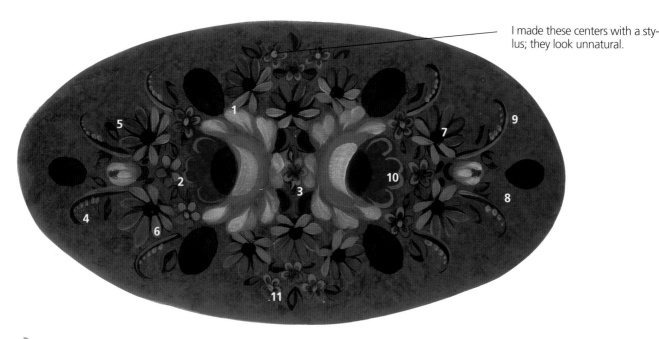

4 With Naples Yellow Hue and a no. 2 and mini filbert, highlight the roses and buds (1). Mix Brilliant Violet and Unbleached Titanium and stroke inner violet petals with a mini filbert (2). Deepen the violet details with Dioxazine Purple using a 10/0 round (3). With Yellow Oxide and a 10/0 round, add the lily background (4). Add Trans Magenta to the back echinacea petals with a mini filbert (5). Add Red Violet mixed with Naples Yellow Hue to the front echinacea petals with a mini filbert (6). Add Purple Madder centers with a mini filbert (7). Using a 10/0 round, apply the leaf details with Green Oxide (8). Highlight the lily stems with Moss Green and a 10/0 round (9). Mix Purple Madder and Unbleached Titanium and highlight the back rose petals with a 10/0 round (10). Add Yellow Oxide centers to the violets with a 10/0 round (11).

5 Use Moss Green and a 10/0 round to highlight the leaves (1). With Unbleached Titanium and a 10/0 round, highlight the roses (2). Define the rose bowl with a 10/0 liner and Purple Madder (3). With a small stylus and Norwegian Orange, add the echinacea centers (4). Using Naples Yellow Hue and a 10/0 round, add highlights throughout the design as shown (5). Mix a little Yellow Oxide with Purple Madder to make a "weed" mix. (Typically on a Russian palette, the weed mix is all of the leftover paint mixed together). Use a 10/0 round to add the weeds (6). Lighten the weeds with Yellow Oxide mixed with a touch of Purple Madder. Apply with a 10/0 round (7). Allow to dry, then wipe with a damp cloth and spray with three to four coats of Krylon Crystal Clear Acrylic Spray to get the lacquered look of a Russian tray.

Use the same techniques if you wish to paint a duck decoy like mine.

Khokhloma Candlesticks and Candy Dish

*a*nother fascinating form of art from Russia is Golden Khokhloma (pronounced Hok-lo-ma). This 300-year-old art form uses a faux gilding technique.

The traditional process takes anywhere from two to four months. First, the wooden piece is made and kiln dried. Next, a thin layer of clay primer is applied to the piece. When this is dry, three coats of oil are applied to make the piece sticky. It is then "tinned" with powdered aluminum and kiln dried once more; this leaves a silver finish on the piece. An artist then handpaints it, using mostly fruit, floral and bird motifs. When the painting is finished, a lacquer is applied and any areas left unpainted turn to "gold."

Hopefully, it won't take you that long to paint this project. When you consider all that takes place in creating the real thing, it does make you appreciate it all the more.

Paint Mixes

We haven't done much paint mixing up till now, but this time I wanted to tone the main colors down a little, so I've included some paint mixes in the color palette at right. You don't need to mix these colors until you're ready to paint the design. Use a bent palette knife to mix them, and add a little flow medium to each to keep them smooth.

Actually, the colors used in traditional Khokhloma look a little brighter than mine. You can leave yours on the brighter side if you wish—just be careful they're not too garish!

SURFACES
- two 6¾-inch (17.2cm) candlesticks
- 7-inch (17.8cm) wooden bowl

ADDITIONS TO BASIC SUPPLIES
- soft cloth
- Krylon Ultra Flat Black Spray, no. 1602 (optional)

BRUSHES
- ¾-inch (19mm) wash brush
- no. 6 and no. 8 flats
- mini, no. 2 and no. 4 filberts
- 10/0 scroller
- 10/0 Dressden liner
- 10/0 and no. 0 round

COLOR PALETTE

Jo Sonja's Rich Gold

Jo Sonja's Yellow Oxide

Jo Sonja's Moss Green

Jo Sonja's Cadmium Scarlet

Jo Sonja's Olive Green

Jo Sonja's Carbon Black

Cadmium Scarlet (fifty-cent-piece-size puddle) + touch of Olive Green = red mix

Rich Gold + touch of Yellow Oxide + touch of Moss Green + touch of Olive Green = gold mix

one part Yellow Oxide + one part Moss Green + one part Olive Green = green mix

Preparing the Surfaces

1 This look is very smooth and shiny. It's important to fill and sand the wood properly. There is usually a big screw hole at the bottom of the candlesticks. Tighten the screws, then fill the hole with wood filler. It will take at least a day for the filler to dry.

2 Sand smooth when dry.

3 Follow wood prep steps on page 14. Dry overnight.

4 Base the candlesticks and dish with flat black spray or brushed-on Carbon Black acrylic. Apply two to three coats, sanding between coats with an extra-fine 3M Sanding Sponge.

INNER BOWL DESIGN

INNER GOLD MOTIF
Trace for gold mix.

INNER BOWL SCALLOPS
Trace for red mix.

The designs on pages 112-113 may be hand-traced or photocopied for personal use only. Enlarge this pattern 111% on a photocopier to return to full size.

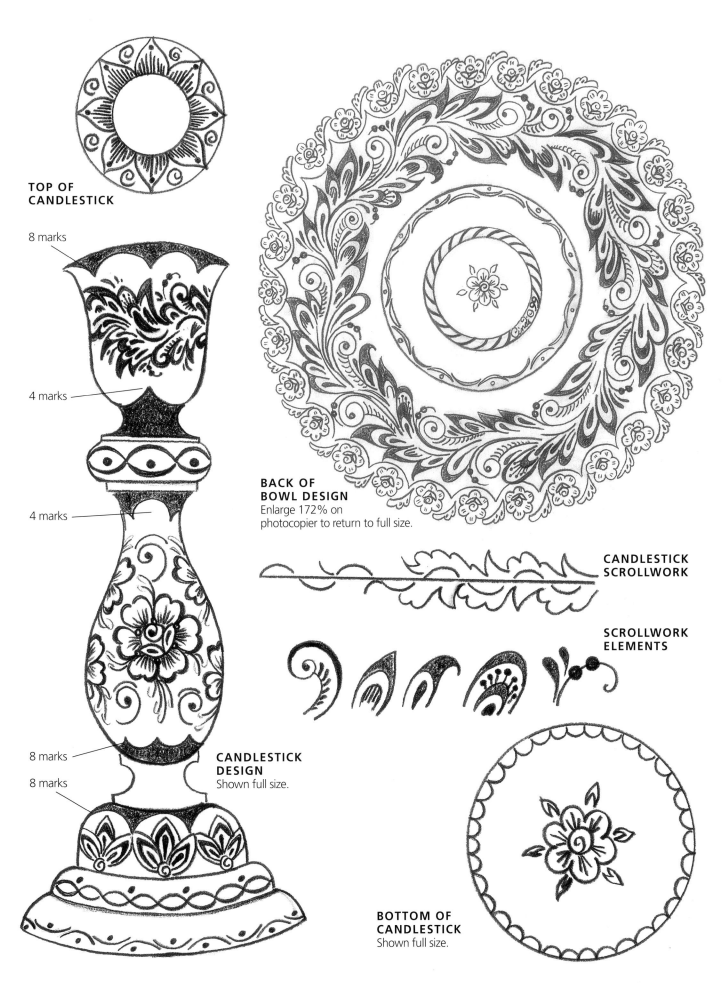

TOP OF CANDLESTICK

8 marks

4 marks

4 marks

8 marks

8 marks

CANDLESTICK DESIGN
Shown full size.

BACK OF BOWL DESIGN
Enlarge 172% on photocopier to return to full size.

CANDLESTICK SCROLLWORK

SCROLLWORK ELEMENTS

BOTTOM OF CANDLESTICK
Shown full size.

1 *Painting the Inside of the Bowl*

Copy only the outline of the inner bowl scallops and inner gold motif from page 112 to tracing paper. Cut a circle around the pattern and use the chalk method to transfer just the scallop design to the bowl. Dust off. Paint the scallops all the way around the bowl with the red mix on a no. 8 flat. The best way to keep this smooth is to paint one scallop at a time, then blend in toward the middle and smooth as you go. When the first coat is dry, you can smooth out any ridges with an extra-fine 3M Sanding Sponge, then wipe with a damp cloth. Apply a second coat and allow to dry (1). Match the pattern over the painted scallops and transfer the inner gold motif. Dust off. Paint these scallops with the gold mix on a no. 8 or no. 6 flat, smoothing as you go. Dry, then apply a second coat. With a no. 2 filbert, paint the three upper leaves and the swirl underneath with two coats of the gold mix (2). Using the scallops and gold motif as a guide, mark off the rim with white chalk as shown by the blue marks (3). To paint the tulips, load a no. 2 filbert with the gold mix. Paint the middle stroke first, followed by the two side strokes. Then, with a no. 0 round, add an **S**-stroke to each side. Paint the three-leaf motif between each tulip using a no. 2 filbert or a no. 0 round. Apply two coats of gold mix to all of these areas (4). With a no. 2 filbert and a no. 10/0 liner, paint details with the green mix as shown (5). With thinned Carbon Black and a 10/0 round, 10/0 liner and 10/0 scroller, paint the outlines as shown (6). Add the petal shadow lines with Carbon Black (7). Using a 10/0 liner and a 10/0 round with Carbon Black, outline the tulips and add the details (8). Outline the leaves and detail in the same manner (9). With the red mix and a 10/0 liner, add strokes and dots (10). Add the gold details using the gold mix and a 10/0 round (11).

> ### ❧ Hint ❧
> I'll continue to show you how to complete the inside of the bowl here. However, since you'll need the chalk marks from the rim to mark off the back of the bowl, it's best at this point to flip the bowl over and finish the back first. Skip to step two, then come back to this step to finish the inside.

Use a no. 0 round and the gold mix to go around the inner rim (12). Use a no. 0 round and the red mix to go around the outer rim (13). With a 10/0 round and Carbon Black, add **S**-strokes over the gold band (14). With a 10/0 scroller and the gold mix, add chain **S**-strokes over the red band (15). Use a small stylus to add little dots on every other chain (16).

2 Painting the Outside of the Bowl

Base the outside of the bowl with the red mix. The outside of the bowl will go a lot faster if you mark it off freehand. You can transfer the design, but it might take longer due to the curve of the bowl. Use white chalk to extend the marks from the rim. Between each line make a light circle using a template and chalk pencil—these will help you make the flowers and scallops. Next, form scallops above the circles using chalk or a chalk pencil (chalk pencil is harder to remove) (1). Using the red mix plus flow medium and a no. 8 or no. 6 flat, paint around the scallops. Start and end each stroke at the point between the scallops (2). Keep the mix a little thin and smooth the ridges down as you go. Use a ¾-inch (19mm) wash brush to finish basecoating up to the base of the bowl after the scallops are edged in. If any ridges have formed, sand lightly with a 3M Sanding Sponge when dry. Wipe with a damp cloth, then give this area a second coat. Allow to dry. Divide the bowl in half with chalk (3). Then draw a line from

the center through every other scallop (4). Draw the top half of an oval between every other set of lines (5). Draw the bottom half of an oval between the remaining sets of lines (6). Add a little "tail" to the end of the ovals, reversing every other one (7). Now you have a foundation for the scrollwork. At first the scrollwork pattern looks overwhelming, but when you break it down it becomes much easier. Follow my examples with chalk, then you'll be ready to paint (8). To paint the scrolls use the gold mix and a no. 4 filbert (9). When dry, apply a second coat. Dry. Paint the half oval lines back in over the gold using the red mix and a 10/0 liner (10). This gives the scrolls even more definition. Using Carbon Black thinned with flow medium, add the details as shown using a 10/0 scroller, 10/0 liner, 10/0 round, stylus and an EZ Dotz tool or the end of your brush handles (11). With a no. 2 filbert and the gold mix, paint the top three petals of all of the flowers around the edge of the bowl (12). Next, go around the edge adding all of the bottom petals (13). The flowers will be more consistent if you do one section at a time all the way around the

bowl. Repeat the last two steps to give the flowers a second coat. Define the flowers by outlining them with Carbon Black and a 10/0 round (14). Add the middle details in the same manner (15). Add the rest of the border strokes using a 10/0 round and the gold mix as shown (16-18). Start the flower in the middle of the base (shown above) the same way you did those on the border, using a no. 2 filbert and the gold mix (19). Use a 10/0 round and Carbon Black to paint the center "creases" in the flower, then add the center swirl and leaves with a 10/0 round (20). Using a no. 0 round and the gold mix, paint a band around the flower. With a 10/0 liner, make **S**-strokes over the band as shown (21). Paint the border around the base with the gold mix and a 10/0 liner as shown. Use a small stylus for dots (22).

3 Painting the Candlesticks

Once you've mastered the bowl, painting the candlestick should go pretty quickly. Again, it's easier to mark off the design than trace the pattern. Hopefully after this lesson, you should feel confident coming up with your own designs and painting them freehand. First, mark off the candlestick with chalk as shown on page 113. Divide the areas into four or eight sections as indicated:

• Divide the top section in half, then in half again. Now divide each fourth again and you will have eight marks.

• Move down to the next section and divide in half, then half again, lining the marks up with the top section.

• Move down to the next section and divide into fourths, setting the marks between the above marks.

• The next section is divided in eighths. Line these marks up with the marks in the section above.

• The last set also has eight marks, again lined up with the section above.

To paint the scallops, just follow the marks—the scallop points down at each mark. Using a no. 6 flat and the red mix, start at the top and work your way down, filling in the red areas (1). Use a little flow medium to keep the paint smooth. Apply two coats and allow to dry. With a chalk pencil, lightly divide the top red section in half horizontally (2). Using the marks as guidelines, draw in half ovals, reversing every other one (3). Finish drawing in the scrolls as shown on page 117, then base with two coats of the gold mix on a mini filbert. Using a 10/0 liner and the gold mix, paint the gold bands (4). Using a 10/0 liner, paint the strokes in the second section as shown (5). Add stylus dots with the green mix (6). Evenly mark off spots for the flowers using chalk. Using a no. 2 filbert and the gold mix, base in the flowers. Apply two coats (7). With the gold mix and a no. 6 flat, paint the large band (8). Paint the leaves with a no. 0 round and two coats of the gold mix (9). With a 10/0 liner, paint an **S**-chain as shown using the gold mix. Add dots with a stylus (10). Paint the bottom ring using a no. 6 flat and the gold mix (11). Leave the base black.

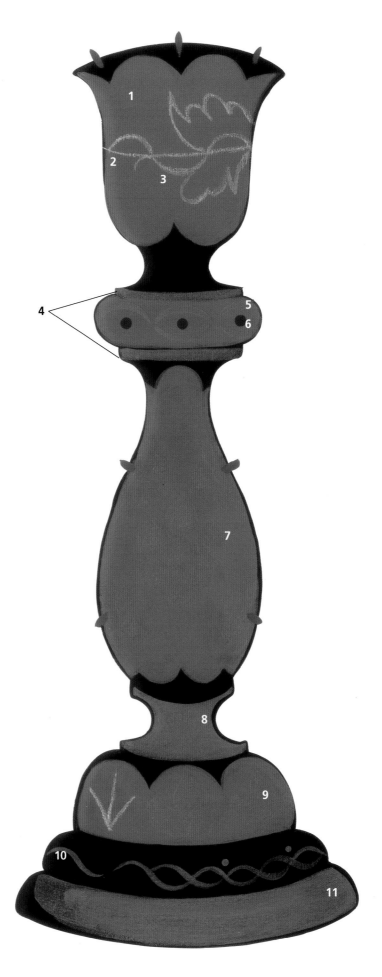

4 Finishing the Red Sections on the Candlestick

In this illustration I've combined the red sections from the top, middle and bottom of the candlestick to give you a quick overview of how to finish the details. Refer back to the bowl steps for more detailed instructions. With the red mix and a 10/0 round, repaint the half oval lines on the top section of scrollwork (1). Using a 10/0 round and Carbon Black, finish the details. Use a stylus for the dots (2). Add gold mix strokes by the flowers as shown, using a 10/0 round (3). Using Carbon Black and a 10/0 round, add the creases and outline the petals (4). Add the flower centers and shadow under the strokes with a 10/0 round and Carbon Black (5). Use a stylus to paint Carbon Black dots on each petal, then go over the dots with smaller gold mix stylus dots (6). With a no. 2 filbert and gold mix, paint swirls between the flowers (7). Add detail to the swirls using a 10/0 liner and Carbon Black (8). Using the green mix and a 10/0 liner, outline the leaves (9). Add a green mix dot to the center of the leaves with a stylus. Add inner details to the leaves and a little swirl to the dot with a 10/0 round and Carbon Black (10).

5 The Candlestick Top

Paint a circle centered at each of the eight marks you made, using a no. 2 filbert and two coats of the gold mix (1). With a 10/0 round and Carbon Black, stroke over the edges of the circle to form a point. Paint over the gold areas outside the point (2). Add a stylus dot with Carbon Black. Use a 10/0 round for the creases (3). Add gold mix swirls with a 10/0 round (4).

6 Finishing the Candy Dish and Candlestick

The flower in the center of the base of the candlestick is the same as the one on the bottom of the bowl. I used a no. 2 filbert and the gold mix to make quick little scallops using the shape of the brush. Once everything is dry, wipe off all chalk marks and dust with a damp cloth. Spray lightly with three to four coats of Krylon Crystal Clear Acrylic Spray, allowing it to dry between coats. Wax if desired after twenty-four hours.

Holiday Ornaments

Seasonal painting always sparks new ideas for me. I've painted a few hundred glass ball ornaments over the years; included in this project are three classics that always sell well and aren't too hard to make. I hope the little scene on the sled will add a special glow to your holidays.

Preparing the Sled and Bell

1 Follow the instructions for wood prep on page 14.

2 You can basecoat with three light coats of Krylon Hooker's Green spray paint or brush on two to three coats of Deep River Green mixed with a little flow medium. The spray is easier to get into the little corners.

3 If you use a satin finish spray, apply a coat of Krylon Matte Finish Spray, no. 1311 after the paint is dry so the design will go on more easily.

Preparing the Glass Ornaments

1 Glass ornaments are very fragile. Dry them where nobody can knock them over. Ornaments have a tendency to jump out of your hands, so paint over a towel or other soft material and carpeting. Make sure your hands are steady—don't drink too much coffee!

2 Making an "ornament holder" will make drying your ornaments a lot easier. Divide the Styrofoam lid so you can space the ornaments evenly without touching. Mark the positions, then sharpen the pencils, dip the points in Aleene's Tacky Glue and poke them into the Styrofoam, point down. Carefully remove the metal tops of the ornaments by pinching the little loop

and slide the hole in the ornaments down over the pencils. Don't leave the ornaments on the holder for more then three days—I've found that the pencil (even without an eraser) leaves a discolored mark where it touches the ornament

3 The best way I've found to paint the ornaments is to balance them on the tip of your pinky. If your pinky is too big, tape the ornament over a pencil.

COLOR PALETTE FOR BELL AND SLED

Ceramcoat
Pearl Luster Medium

Jo Sonja's
Green Iridescent

Jo Sonja's
Rich Gold

Ceramcoat
Cornsilk Yellow

Ceramcoat
Ice Storm Violet

Ceramcoat
Violet Ice

Ceramcoat
Pale Yellow

Ceramcoat
Calypso Orange

Ceramcoat
Chambray Blue

Americana
Summer Lilac

Americana
Winter Blue

Americana
Cherry Red

Ceramcoat
Mudstone

Americana
Blue Grey Mist

FolkArt
Sterling Blue

Americana
Raw Sienna

Accent
Classical Bronze

Ceramcoat
Brown Velvet

Americana
Holly Green

Ceramcoat
Lime Green

Americana
Plantation Pine

Ceramcoat
Deep River Green

Ceramcoat
Black Green

"CUT GLASS"
ORNAMENT DESIGN
front

"CUT GLASS"
ORNAMENT
DESIGN
bottom

SLED DESIGN

SLED
RUNNER
DESIGN

POINSETTIA
ORNAMENT
DESIGN

Come
Worship
The King!

Jesus

These designs may be hand-traced or photo-copied for personal use only. Enlarge sled and runner at 125% to return to full size. Ball ornaments shown at full size.

NATIVITY ORNAMENT
DESIGN

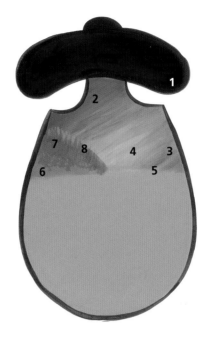

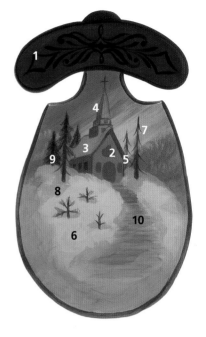

1 *The Sled*

Paint the upper third of the sled face with a no. 10 flat and two to three coats of Pale Yellow. With a ¾-inch (19mm) wash brush give the bottom two-thirds two to three coats of Winter Blue. Using a no. 6 flat moistened with retarder and blotted, apply Sterling Blue over the yellow as shown. Let dry a few minutes.

2

Give the top of the sled and runners three coats of Cherry Red with a no. 10 flat. This is a transparent color; the green underneath will give it an antiqued look (1). You won't see a lot of the background so don't spend a lot of time on it. Deepen the sky with a no. 6 flat and Sterling Blue, working from the edge inward (2). Wipe your brush on a napkin, add a touch of retarder, then pick up Summer Lilac and blend into the Sterling Blue (3). Clean your brush off slightly, load with Calypso Orange and, starting from the middle, work into the previous sky colors (4). With a dirty brush, add a little Pale Yellow and blend in (5). After the sky is established, add the hills using Mudstone on a no. 6 flat (6). Double load your no. 6 flat with Summer Lilac (top) and Sterling Blue. Starting from the edge, hold the brush straight up and pounce in the distant trees (7). Double load again with Calypso Orange (top) and Sterling Blue. Add a few high-lighted trees toward the top middle (8).

3

Copy the sled design to tracing paper. Cut out. Using the chalk method, transfer the church, trees and snow and the handle design. Dust off. Use a 10/0 liner and Black Green to line in the handle design (1). Paint the church front with a no. 2 or no. 0 flat and Blue Grey Mist (2). With Mudstone and a no. 0 flat paint the lighter roof, steeple and step areas (3). Make a half-and-half mix of Classical Bronze and Mudstone and use a no. 0 flat and a 20/0 round to paint the church and steeple sides

and add the front windows (4). Use Classical Bronze for the side windows, cross and roof shadow (5). Add snow with Chambray Blue and a no. 2 flat (6). With a 10/0 liner and Classical Bronze, line in the trees (7). Using a half-and-half mix of Sterling Blue and Chambray Blue, paint the snow shadows with a no. 0 flat (8). Pounce in the pine needles with Plantation Pine and a no. 0 flat (9). Add more shadows with Sterling Blue and a no. 0 flat (10).

MATERIALS

SURFACES
- bell with handle
- mini sled
- non-shiny clear, red and midnight blue glass ball ornaments

ADDITIONS TO BASIC SUPPLIES FOR BELL AND SLED
- small chain and jingle bell
- thin, decorative rope to match
- strong glue or glue gun
- small sponge brush
- Krylon Flat or Satin spray paint, Hooker's Green

ADDITIONS TO BASIC SUPPLIES FOR GLASS ORNAMENTS
- small Styrofoam cooler lid
- new pencils with erasers

- two pieces of heavy paper or cardstock
- Glick Ultra-Fine Multi and Soft Yellow Glitters
- Sparkle Glaze
- white and green ribbon (optional)

BRUSHES
- ½-inch (12mm) and ¾-inch (19mm) wash brushes
- no. 0, no. 2, no. 4, no. 6, no. 8 and no. 10 flats
- ¼-inch (6mm) angle
- no. 2 filbert
- no. 0 flat shader
- 6/0, 10/0, 20/0 Dressden liners
- no. 0, no. 10/0 and no. 20/0 rounds

With a 10/0 liner and Raw Sienna, paint over the Black Green design on the handle, allowing some of the Black Green to show through (1). Using Calypso Orange and a 20/0 round, paint in the window lights and cast light on the steps (2). Add Blue Grey Mist to the steeple and path with a 20/0 round (3). With a no. 2 flat, paint more shadows in the snow with Sterling Blue, then start the snow highlights with Violet Ice (4). Put some Chambray Blue on the roof and around the edge of the design (5). Add Cornsilk Yellow highlights with a no. 0 flat (6). Underpaint the pine needles with Black Green using a dry no. 0 flat. With a 20/0 round, add some Black Green to the small trees. Pounce a little more Plantation Pine over the pine needles (7). Add some Ice Storm Violet to the snow. When dry, use the chalk method to transfer the holly design to the sled (or paint it freehand). Base the pinecones with a no. 2 flat and two coats of Black Green (8). Base the holly berries with two coats of Cherry Red and a no. 0 flat (9). Base the holly leaves with a no. 2 flat and Lime Green and Holly Green (10). Use a 20/0 round and Black Green to shade around the holly berries (11). Add pine branches with a 10/0 liner and Brown Velvet (12). Paint the ribbon in with Rich Gold and a no. 0 round (13).

Finish the handle design with Rich Gold on a 10/0 liner (1). Add Black Green details to the branches with a 20/0 round (2). Use Brown Velvet and a 20/0 round to base the pinecone "petals" (3). With Raw Sienna, add a medium highlight to the branches using a 10/0 round (4). Base the pine needles with a 10/0 liner and Deep River Green (5). Highlight the needles with a 20/0 round and a mix of 3 parts Deep River Green to one part Calypso Orange (6). Shade the pine needles with Black Green and a 10/0 round (7). Add Lime Green veins to the Holly Green sides of the holly leaves and Holly Green veins to the Lime Green sides with a 20/0 round. Also use this brush to add Black Green center vein lines and to outline the Holly Green edge. Outline the Lime Green edge with Holly Green (8). Use a 20/0 round to shade the holly berries with a mix of Black Green and Cherry Red. Highlight the berries with a mix of Cherry Red and Calypso Orange (9). Shade the ribbon with Classical Bronze and a 10/0 liner (10). Add more highlight to the pine needles using a 10/0 liner and Calypso Orange (11). Add detail to the windows and door with a 20/0 round and Summer Lilac, Pale Yellow and Classical Bronze (12). Finish the trees by drybrushing, then pouncing with a no. 0 flat and Chambray Blue and Sterling Blue (13). With a 20/0 Dressden, add a Calypso Orange highlight to the steeple, cross, steps, snow, side window reflection and trees—don't overdo it (14). Put Green Iridescent on the holly leaves and pine needles with a 20/0 round. Add some sparkle to the snow, ribbon and trees with Pearl Luster Medium and a 20/0 round. Take a small, damp sponge brush and add gold around the edges.

6 *The Sled Runners*

Transfer the design onto the runners using chalk; dust off (1). Use Black Green and a 10/0 liner to line in the design. Use a stylus for the dots (2). Dry. Overstroke the design with Raw Sienna on a 10/0 liner and stylus (3). Overstroke again with Rich Gold on a 10/0 liner and stylus (4). Go over all edges with a small sponge brush and Rich Gold (5). Rub the edges and swirl the sides to give it all a nice finish.

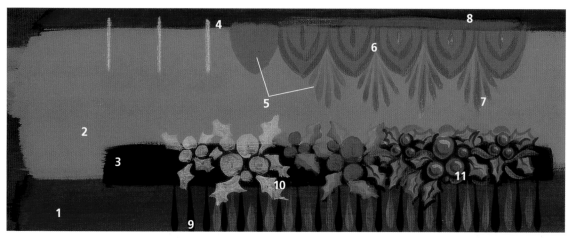

7 *The Bell*

After you've prepared and basecoated the bell, adding the details should go pretty quickly; this design is painted freehand. With a no. 10 flat, give the handle and a 1-inch (2.5cm) band around the bottom two to three coats of Cherry Red mixed with a little flow medium (1). (Do the lip of the bottom but not the inside.) Using Blue Grey Mist and flow medium, paint from the Cherry Red band to the edge of the bell handle with a no. 10 flat (2). Apply two coats. Paint about a ¼-inch (0.6cm) wide Black Green border using a no. 8 flat, overlapping the Cherry Red and Blue Grey Mist edges (3). Using chalk or a chalk pencil, divide the top of the bell into eighths (4). Using a no. 4 flat, paint scallops as shown with Sterling Blue. Using a 10/0 liner, add strokes between the scallops as shown (5). With Rich Gold and a 10/0 liner, overstroke the scallops and strokes as shown and paint a band around the bottom of the handle (6). Using Pearl Luster Medium and a 10/0 liner, add highlights to the Rich Gold overstrokes (7). Paint Holly Green over the gold band at the bottom of the handle, then go over it with Green Iridescent on a 10/0 liner (8). Using Black Green and a 10/0 liner, paint rows of teardrop strokes over the Cherry Red bottom band, then just above the gold and green band on the handle, then at the top of the handle. Leave enough room between each of these strokes to add a Rich Gold stroke (9).

Paint the top of the handle Black Green and add a spiral with Rich Gold. With a 20/0 round and a no. 0 flat, base the holly with Chambray Blue (10). Paint the holly as you did on the sled (11). Add some Rich Gold around the bottom lip of the bell using a small sponge brush.

8 *Finishing*

When all is complete and dry, wipe with a damp cloth, then spray with Krylon Crystal Clear Acrylic Spray. Add rope to the sled and use strong glue to attach the jingle bell and chain to the bell. You could paint this design on an ornament, plate or even on a special card.

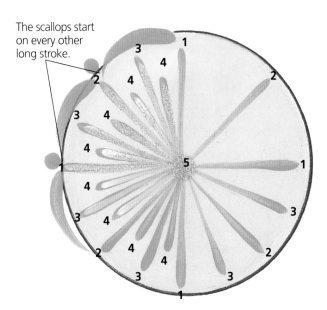

The scallops start on every other long stroke.

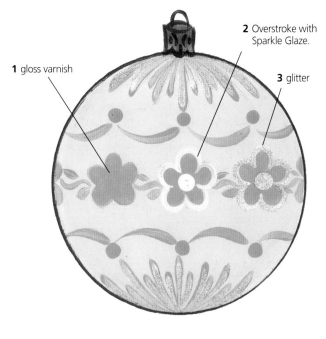

1 gloss varnish

2 Overstroke with Sparkle Glaze.

3 glitter

1 The "Cut Glass" Ornament

When I first started painting on non-shiny ornaments, I discovered by accident that when you put gloss over them, the surface turns transparent. I thought this could be fun, especially when you add Sparkle Glaze and glitter. If you're good at strokework, you'll find this design easy. However, mistakes can't be removed, so you may want to spend some time practicing the strokes on cardstock or posterboard before you begin. Center a 2¼-inch (5.7cm) circle template over the top of the ornament and trace the circle with white chalk or chalk pencil—chalk pencil is very hard to remove so go very lightly if you use it. Repeat on the bottom of the ornament. Divide each circle into fourths. Apply Sparkle Glaze strokes (see below) with a 6/0 liner to one fourth of the design, then, while wet, apply glitter. The Sparkle Glaze acts like glue to hold the glitter to the ornament. Glaze and glitter each section before moving to the next. When you apply the glitter, fold a piece of heavy paper in half, open out and lay under the project to catch the extra glitter. When you're done, use the fold as a funnel to pour the glitter back into the bottle, catching any spills with a second folded sheet. The strokes are applied as follows:

1 Beginning on the bottom of the ornament, apply teardrop strokes that reach the edge of the circle on the fourth marks.

2 Apply another stroke of equal length between the fourth-mark strokes.

3 Apply a shorter stroke on either side of the second stroke—there will be two of these in each fourth.

4 Apply shorter strokes between each of the previous strokes—there will be four of these in each fourth.

5 Place one large dot in the center.

When the bottom is dry, turn the ornament over and repeat on the top. Hold a finger over the hole while you glitter or you'll get glitter inside. Dust off well when dry. After you've finished the top and bottom, apply the scallop borders with a no. 0 round and Jo Sonja's Gloss Varnish. Smooth and shape a Q-tip with your fingers and a little water, then dip it in gloss varnish and paint a dot between each scallop.

2 Stroke in the middle band of flowers, one under each top scallop dot, using a no. 2 filbert and gloss varnish. Don't worry if the flowers don't line up with the bottom dots. Allow to dry. With a 20/0 liner and gloss varnish, paint little **S**-strokes and small leaves between the flowers. Allow to dry. Using Sparkle Glaze and a 20/0 liner, overstroke as shown, then quickly glitter. Use the EZ Dotz tool or the end of a brush handle dipped in Sparkle Glaze for the centers, then glitter. Dry on the ornament holder, then dust loose glitter off. Place the metal top back on and hot glue a small white bow to the top if desired.

COLOR PALETTE FOR "CUT GLASS" ORNAMENT

Ceramcoat Sparkle Glaze

Glick Ultra-Fine Multi Glitter

Jo Sonja's Gloss Varnish (represented by gray in this illustration)

1 marking points

don't crowd

2

leaf strokes

4

3

1

2

1 The Poinsettia Ornament

Remove the metal top and mark off as shown with chalk (1). With Titanium White and a ¼-inch (6mm) angle, make six slight **S**-strokes for the petals, evenly spaced around each mark (2). Double load the brush with Green Oxide and Plum Pink and add the leaves as shown above (3). With a stylus, dot the stamen base in with Green Oxide (4). Allow to dry.

2

Apply Sparkle Glaze over the entire ornament with a ½-inch (12mm) wash brush (1). Place the ornament on the holder and dry for two hours. With a stylus and Taffy Cream, apply the stamen highlights; while wet, add yellow glitter to the stamen (2). Dry for five hours, then dust off excess glitter. Replace the metal top and hot glue a small green bow on if desired

COLOR PALETTE FOR POINSETTIA ORNAMENT

Ceramcoat
Sparkle Glaze

Glick
Ultra-Fine Soft Yellow
Glitter

Jo Sonja's
Titanium White

Americana
Taffy Cream

Jo Sonja's
Green Oxide

Jo Sonja's
Plum Pink

The Nativity Ornament

1 Remove the metal top carefully. You can freehand this design or transfer it using the chalk method. With a no. 4 flat and Brown Iron Oxide, base in the stall (1). Use a no. 2 filbert to apply two coats of Dresden Flesh to the face (2). With a no. 2 filbert and Oyster White plus a little flow medium, stroke on the blanket, allowing the background color to show through for shadows (3). Using thinned Black and a 20/0 liner, add the wood details (4). With a 20/0 round and White, paint in the lettering (5). Using a 20/0 liner and thinned Rich Gold, stroke in the star (6). Add some hay with Territorial Beige and a 20/0 liner (7). With thinned Rich Gold and a 20/0 liner, place pairs of strokes around the design as shown (8). Add pairs of strokes going the opposite direction (9).

2 Add detail to the face with a 20/0 round and Territorial Beige. Use Plum Pink for the lips (1). Add hay details with Antique Gold and Brown Iron Oxide using a 20/0 liner (2). If needed, use a 20/0 liner and Oyster White to outline the blanket (3). Add a little more wood detail using Territorial Beige and Brown Iron Oxide (4). Mix White with a little Black to make gray and use a 20/0 round to paint the nail. With Dresden Flesh and a little Brown Iron Oxide, paint the sign. Use Black and a 20/0 round for the lettering on the sign (5). Add highlight strokes using Bluebonnet and a 20/0 liner (6). Add White overstrokes with a 20/0 liner (7). Make dots on the border with a stylus and Sparkle Glaze and sprinkle with glitter. Using a 20/0 round and Sparkle Glaze, go over the lettering and the White strokes and dots, then quickly add glitter (8). When dry, dust off the extra glitter with a mop brush. Paint the front with J.W. etc. Right-Step Satin Varnish and the back with Sparkle Glaze. Dry overnight. Replace the metal top. You can easily change these colors if you'd like.

COLOR PALETTE FOR NATIVITY ORNAMENT

Ceramcoat
White

Accent
Bluebonnet

Ceramcoat
Antique Gold

Jo Sonja's
Rich Gold

Ceramcoat
Dresden Flesh

Ceramcoat
Black

Ceramcoat
Oyster White

Jo Sonja's
Plum Pink

Ceramcoat
Territorial Beige

Ceramcoat
Brown Iron Oxide

Ceramcoat
Sparkle Glaze

Glick
Ultra-Fine Multi Glitter

RESOURCES

3M
Phone: (651) 737-6501
Web site: www.mmm.com
3M Sanding Sponge and Long-Mask Masking Tape

A Touch of Crafts
P.O. Box 849
Rancho Cucamonga, CA 91730
Web site: www.ezdotz.com
EZ Dotz tool

Artist's Club, The
P.O. Box 8930
Vancouver, WA 98668-8930
Phone: (800) 845-6507
Web site: www.artistsclub.com
Dry-It Board, Glick Glitter and Sta-Wet Palette

Cabin Crafters
P.O. Box 270
Nevada, IA 50201
Phone: (800) 669-3920
Web site: www.cabincrafters.com
wooden bowl #36-071 or #36-401 similar to project 13 bowl

Chroma, Inc.
205 Bucky Dr.
Lititz, PA 17543
Phone (800) 257-8278
Web site: www.chroma-inc.com/josonja/
E-mail: info@chroma-inc.com
Jo Sonja paints and mediums

DecoArt
P.O. Box 327
Stanford, KY 40484
Phone: (606) 365-3193
Fax: (606) 365-9739
Web site: www.decoart.com
E-mail: paint@decoart.com
Americana paints

Delta Technical Coatings, Inc.,
2550 Pellissier Place
Whittier, CA 90601
Phone: (800) 423-4135
Fax: (562) 695-5157
Web site: www.deltacrafts.com
Ceramcoat paints

Dux' Dekes Decoy Company
1356 North Rd.
Greenwich, NY 12834
Phone and fax: (692-7703)
Toll free phone: (800) 553-4725

Web site: www.duxdekes.com
E-mail: duxdekes@capital.net
wooden duck decoy similar to project 12

General Pencil Co., Inc.
P.O. Box 531
Redwood City, CA 94063
Phone: (650) 369-4889
Fax: (650) 369-7169
Web site: www.generalpencil.com
"The Masters" Brush Cleaner and Preserver

Jo Ann Stores, Inc.
Web site: www.joann.com
project 14 non-shiny glass ball ornaments

J.W. etc.
2205 First St., Suite 103
Simi Valley, CA 93065
Phone: (805) 526-5066
Fax: (805) 526-1297
Web site: www.jwetc.com
E-mail: jwetc@earthlink.net
J.W. etc. products

Koh-I-Noor Inc.
100 North St.
Bloomsbury, NJ 08804
Phone: (800) FINE ART
Accent paints

Krylon
Phone: (800) 4 KRYLON
Web site: www.krylon.com
Krylon spray finishes, primers and paints

Loew-Cornell
563 Chestnut Ave.
Teaneck, NJ 07666-2490
Phone: (201) 836-7070
Fax: (201) 836-8110
Web site: www.loew-cornell.com
E-mail: loew-cornell@loew-cornell.com
Super Chacopaper

Michaels Stores, Inc.
P.O. Box 619566
DFW, TX 75261-9566
Phone: (972) 409-1300
Web site: www.michaels.com
general craft supplies, Krylon sprays, project 1 candle, project 2 papier-mâché heart box, project 3 card box and tiny bean pot, Walnut Hollow wooden tea set similar to project 4, project 7 hat pin box and earring and pin backs, project 14 sled

Plaid Enterprises, Inc.
ATTN: Customer Service
P.O. Box 2835
Norcross, GA 30091-2835
Phone: (800) 842-4197
Web site: www.plaidonline.com
E-mail: talk@plaidonline.com
FolkArt paints, Soft Flock

Scharff Brushes, Inc.
P.O. Box 746
Fayetteville, GA 30214
Phone: (888) SCHARFF or (770) 461-2200
Fax: (770) 461-2472
Web site: www.artbrush.com
E-mail: scharff@artbrush.com
My favorite brushes—please mention this book when calling for information or ordering

Tru-Color Systems
P.O. Box 486
Danville, IN 46122-0486
Phone: (317) 745-7535
Fax: (317) 745-1886
Web site: www.tru-color.com
T.C.S. Decorative Painting Color Match Sourcebook *for converting my paint colors to other brands*

Vesterheim Norwegian-American Museum
P.O. Box 379
Decorah, IA 52101-0379
Phone (800) 979-3346
Web site: www.vesterheim.org
E-mail: vesterheim@vesterheim.org
project 1 key chain; project 2 wooden puffed hearts; project 3 heart-shaped box and small pill box #57; project 10 needle box, spools and thimble; project 13 candlesticks; and project 14 bell with handle #49

Zim's, Inc.
4370 South 300 West
Salt Lake City, UT 84107-2630
Phone: (801) 268-2505
project 9 double switch plate #A-604 and project 11 nesting dolls, set D

INDEX